KV-061-564

	UNIT TITLE	VOCABULARY: TOPICS/ DEVELOPMENT	GRAMMAR	FUNCTIONS
9	**Skin deep**	T: People's appearances T: Models and model agencies T: Ideas of beauty D: Adjectives describing people D: Compound adjectives and prepositional phrases	*Look* + adjective *Look like* + noun *Must, can't, might, could* + *be*	Certainty and probability in the future Guessing Making deductions
	Progress check			
10	**Showtime**	T: Puppets T: Theatre T: Circuses T: Animal performers D: Related words D: Negative prefixes	*Be able* + *to* + infinitive *Manage* + *to* + infinitive *Can* and *could*	Talking about achievement Making requests/deductions Expressing ability/possibility Giving permission Talking about prohibition Giving opinions
	Talkback			
11	**Looking forward**	T: Energy sources T: Life in the future T: Life in a closed ecosystem T: Genetic engineering D: The prefix *self-* D: Compound adjectives (time and size)	*Will* + (adverb) + infinitive *Going to* + infinitive *May/might* + infinitive Articles	Making decisions, promises, predictions Expressing plans and intentions Asking for explanations Introducing examples Interrupting Talking about certainty, probability, possibility, plans and ideas
	Progress check			
12	**News and views**	T: Newspapers T: Objectivity and bias in newspapers T: Reading habits T: Perspectives on events D: Adjectives and their connotations	Past simple passive Present perfect passive	
	Talkback			
13	**On show**	T: Exhibitions and museums T: Art T: Children and childhood D: *Go* + adjective D: Words with similar and opposite meanings	Past perfect simple	Asking for and giving directions Describing location/people Interpreting/inferring from pictures Expressing opinions and feelings Hesitating
	Progress check			
14	**In touch**	T: Couriers T: Emergency services T: Home computers D: Verbs for reporting results	Reported speech	Telephoning Use of tenses in sections of a report
	Talkback			
15	**A change of scene**	T: Preparations for travel T: Working holidays/Holidays T: Persuasion T: Travel brochures D: Adjectives: degrees of intensity	First conditional Conjunctions: *if, unless, when, as soon as* Indirect questions Embedded questions	Asking politely
	Progress check			
	Exercises for Student B			
↻	**Comparing cultures**	Housing, *page 13*. Postcards, *page 28*. Theft and punishment, *page 33*. At the doctor's, *page 50*. Words describing sounds, *page 52*. Education, *page 65*.		

AHEAD
L O O K
classroom
COURSE

…diate

…OK

…IS

…ER

…ership between

…dge Local
…ate (UCLES)

 with the cooperation of the Council of Europe

Longman

Welcome to Look Ahead Intermediate

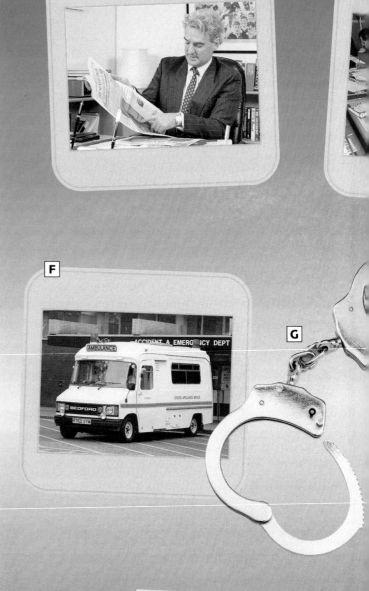

A

1 Discuss the pictures.

1 What do you think the people in Pictures A to E do?
2 What are the objects in Pictures F to J? Where would you see them?
3 Describe the texts in Pictures K to O. What is their purpose? Who would normally read them?

2 Match each person with an object and a text.

3 Work in pairs to match the pictures and texts with unit titles.

Student A: Look at this page and describe the pictures to your partner.

Student B: Turn to the contents chart on pages 2 to 5 and identify the five unit titles that the pictures relate to.

4 Discuss your answers with another pair of students. Do you all agree?

5 ▣ Listen to extracts from interviews with the people in Pictures A to E. Which person is talking in each of the five extracts? Were you correct about their work?

F

G

K

PRACTICAL
WAYS
TO CRACK
CRIME
THE
FAMILY GUIDE

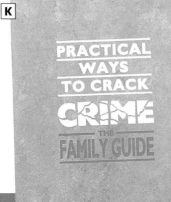

L

HORSE

PARKING
ONLY

ALL OTHERS
TOWED
AWAY

©1991 KAY-JO ENT.   HORSEMENS ORD. 1- 505-758-0058

Changes

Focus

GETTING STARTED

1 Look at these pictures of an area of London called 'Docklands'.

1 Which years do you think the pictures are from?
   about 1910   the 1970s   the 1990s
2 What sort of area is Docklands now? What sort of area do you think it was in the past?

LISTENING

2 📼 Listen to the cassette and check your answers to question 2 in Exercise 1.

READING

3 Read these people's memories of life in Docklands in the past. Match the topics with the texts.

WORK   PLEASURE   HOME
THE RIVER

A The river was magical, especially when you were only eight years old. You could travel to any place in the world just by looking at the different ships that passed. There were ships of all sizes and nationalities. There were tugs, police launches, sailing barges and, of course, the river buses. In those days the river was alive.

B The park was the centre of our fun. We never used to have toys – we depended on our imagination. On Monday evenings during the summer we often went to see film shows from a travelling van, and sometimes there was a conjuror who pulled rabbits out of hats. My clearest memory is of Saturday evenings when we always went to the park with other families to see the pleasure boats returning from their trips to the seaside.

C We had a bedroom and a living room upstairs in my grandmother's house. There was no hot water or anything. We used to go out to the wash-house in the back garden to fill up the watering can. That used to be our domestic water, for washing, cooking, even bathing.

D My father was a stevedore: he used to load and unload the ships. Dad often used to come home from the docks without any work. Mum used to cry, and poor old Dad didn't say a word. A lot of stevedores paid the foreman to get a day's work. Dad didn't use to pay, so he didn't get work every day. Money was always a problem.

4 Find information in the texts to support or contradict these statements about Docklands in the past.

1 Docklands was a rich area.
2 People were very friendly with their neighbours.
3 The river played an important role in people's lives.

5 Look for words and phrases in the texts.

1 What names are there for different kinds of boats? Which ones carried members of the public as passengers?
2 What are the words for these jobs?
   a) a person who performs magic tricks
   b) a person who works at the docks
   c) a person who is responsible for other people at work

DISCOVERING LANGUAGE

6 Look at this sentence and answer the questions.

My father used to load and unload the ships.

1 Which of these verb forms can replace *used to load and unload*?
   a) is going to load and unload
   b) loads and unloads
   c) loaded and unloaded
   Does *used to* refer to the future, present or past?
2 Is it probable that the man does the same job now? What is the special meaning of *used to*?
3 What part of speech follows *used to* in a sentence?
4 Find other examples of *used to* in the texts. What are its two negative forms?
5 *Used to* behaves like a regular verb. Complete this question with the question form:
   ..... you ..... enjoy life in Docklands?

7 Work in pairs. Ask your partner about his/her childhood. Ask about home, school, free time, family holidays and anything else you can think of. Start like this:

Where did you use to live?

Make notes and be ready to tell the class about your partner.

🔊 Documentary

LISTENING

8 Before you listen, check the meaning of these words in a dictionary.

skilled *(adj)*   purchase *(v)*   sink *(v)*   estate *(n)*
deserted *(adj)*   thrive *(v)*   row *(n)*   spirit *(n)*
professional *(adj)*

Now add each word to one or more of these phrases to show possible contexts.

1 a ..... of houses   6 ..... workers
2 a ..... job   7 plants that ..... in forests
3 to ..... a flat   8 ships that ..... at sea
4 a ..... building   9 a modern housing .....
5 the ..... of our time

9 📼 Listen to Terry Ward, who has worked in the Docklands area for years.

1 Make notes about Docklands now, using these headings:
   JOBS
   WEEKENDS
   COMMUNITY LIFE
2 Terry also talks about the way Docklands used to be. What do we learn from him that we did not learn from the texts in Exercise 3?

WRITING

10 Write sentences comparing Docklands as it was and as it is now.

People in Docklands used to ... , but now ... .

SPEAKING

11 Are there areas in your country that have changed as dramatically as Docklands? Are they better or worse now than in the past? Give reasons for your opinions.

Moving on

1 Think about times in the past when your life changed.

1 Did you plan the changes? Did you have to make important decisions?
2 Were there any big changes that you did not plan?

Focus

TOPIC
• Changes in lifestyles

GRAMMAR
• Present simple
• Adverbs of frequency
• Present progressive for current events
• Present progressive for fixed future plans

FUNCTIONS
• Greetings
• Asking/talking about health
• Introductions
• Responding to introductions

SKILLS
• Reading: an article
• Listening: short conversations
• Speaking: role play

VOCABULARY DEVELOPMENT
• Compound nouns (noun + noun)

SPEECH PATTERNS
• Stress in compound nouns

READING

2 Before you read, look at this picture and the title of the article. Describe the picture in detail. What do you think the article is about? Read it and check.

3 Guess the meaning of these words from their context in the article. Then check with a dictionary.

skips   left-over   mortgage   pension

4 Discuss answers to these questions.

1 Where do Andrew's possessions come from?
2 Why does he live like this?
3 What does he do with things that he does not need?
4 How did he use to live?
5 Do you think he is happier now than he used to be?
6 What do you think of his lifestyle?

A flatful of rubbish

Andrew Weston-Webb is sitting in his tiny one-room flat with other people's rubbish all around him. He is wearing someone else's clothes and someone
5- else's shoes. He hardly ever buys new things. Instead, he goes out at night and looks through skips left by builders at the side of the road. He found most of his things in a skip somewhere in the city: his
10- bookshelves, his armchair, the lamps and lampshades, the books, the old records, the paintings and the coat hooks on his walls. He even has a set of playing cards that he made from used phone cards.
15-   There is a philosophy behind his lifestyle. Andrew cares for the environment by using other people's waste. When he does not want things any more, he sells them to other people at
20- street markets. 'I tell them the whole story and pass on my message. People love it.'

Andrew is going down to the fruit and vegetable market later today to get some left-over food, and tonight he is going on another night-time search. His life was not -25 always like this. He used to be an executive with British Telecom and he lived in a large house in the suburbs. But that is all in the past. 'Who wants a mortgage on your home and a pension for -30 your old age? I feel much happier living here. Life's an adventure this way.' ■

DEVELOPING VOCABULARY

5 Look at examples of compound nouns from the article.

bookshelves   armchair   lampshades   coat hooks   phone cards
street markets   night-time

1 What is a compound noun? In these examples, what part of speech is each part of the compound?
2 These words can replace the first part of some of the compounds above. Which ones?
   identity   day   vegetable   fish   curtain   kitchen   bed
3 Can you make any new compounds by changing the *second* part of the examples above?   *phone book*

SPEECH PATTERNS

6 🔊 Listen to the compound nouns from Exercise 5.

1 Mark the main stress on each compound. Can you see a pattern?
2 Listen again and repeat.

DISCOVERING LANGUAGE

7 Read these sentences from the article.

A *He goes out at night and looks through skips …*
B *He is wearing someone else's clothes …*
C *… tonight he is going on another night-time search.*

1 Which sentence refers to:
   a) a fixed plan for the future?   b) a present routine?
   c) a present and temporary activity?
2 Which tense is used to express each of these meanings? Find other examples in the article.

8 Look again at the first paragraph of the article.

1 Which expression completes this sentence in the text? What does the sentence mean?
   He ..... buys new things.
2 What other adverbs of frequency are common with present simple verbs? Use them to complete the same sentence.
   He **never** buys new things.

SPEAKING

9 Work in pairs. Discuss the differences between your lifestyle and Andrew's. Compare your clothes, homes, possessions and routines. What questions would you like to ask Andrew about his way of life?

10 Continue to work with your partner.

Student A: Take the role of Andrew. Respond to your partner as you think he would.
Student B: Be yourself. Imagine that you meet Andrew at a street market. Greet him, introduce yourself and tell him you know about him. Then ask questions about his lifestyle and the goods he has to sell.

FOCUS ON FUNCTIONS

11 How did you greet Andrew? Think about different situations that you find yourself in in your own country.

1 How do you greet friends and introduce them to each other? How do you greet and introduce people more formally?
2 Write English phrases that you know under these headings:
   GREETINGS   INTRODUCTIONS
   Which phrases are informal? Which ones are more formal?
3 Do you dress and behave differently in more formal situations?

LISTENING

12 🔊 Listen to two conversations. A woman is meeting people in two different situations.

1 Which conversation is formal? Which one is informal?
2 Look at your lists from Exercise 11 and tick the phrases that you hear. Add any other phrases to your lists.

SPEAKING

13 Work in groups of four and role play this situation. You have arrived for a weekend course.

Student A: You are the course leader. Greet people and introduce them to each other.
Student B: You are a student. You only know C.
Student C: You are also a student. You are surprised and pleased that B is here.
Student D: You are a teacher arriving for the course. You know A.

When you have finished, change roles.

Focus

TOPIC
• Housing

FUNCTIONS
• Describing
  location/people/
  buildings

SKILLS
• Listening: a
  description
• Speaking: a
  description
• Writing: gap-filling

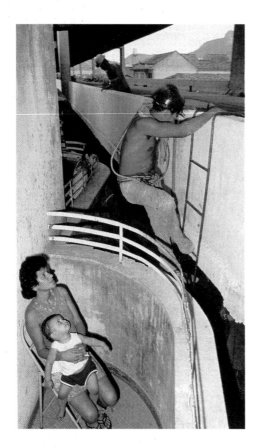

Describing pictures

GETTING STARTED

**1 Look at these pictures of different types of homes.
Then read the questionnaire below.**

1 Which of the homes matches the information in the
   questionnaire?
2 Now copy and complete the questionnaire with
   information about your home.
3 Ask your partner about his/her home.

> **QUESTIONNAIRE**
> 1 Is your home a flat … a house … other (please specify) .✓. ? *cave*
> 2 Is the building detached .✓. semi-detached … terraced … a block of flats … ?
> 3 Is it modern … more than 50 years old … very old .✓. ?
> 4 Is it made of brick … stone .✓. wood … concrete … other (please specify) … ?
> 5 Is the roof made of tiles … slates … other (please specify) .✓. ? *rock*
> 6 Is the outside of the building in good condition .✓. shabby … in poor
>   condition … ?
> 7 Are there any special features on the outside of the building (e.g. a balcony, a
>   chimney, a porch) .✓. ? *chimney, a television aerial*

4 🔊 **Work in groups of three. Listen again. Choose one of these questions each and make notes.**

1 Which words does the speaker use to describe:
   a) the building?
   b) the people?
   c) the surrounding area?

2 Which nouns does he use with the words and phrases below?
   a) in front (of)   f) at the side (of)
   b) above   g) below
   c) on top (of)   h) a long way (from)
   d) in the centre (of) i) between
   e) at the back (of)   j) close (to)

3 Which words and phrases does he use to say that he is or is not certain about something?   *I should think ...*

Now help each other to describe the same picture.

⟳ COMPARING CULTURES

2 Look at the pictures again.

1 Can you identify the types of building in each picture? Use the words below to help you.
   The picture on the left/on the right/in the middle shows ...
   a house   a tent   a cottage
   a cave   a mobile home
   a houseboat   a hut
   a block of flats   a caravan
   a farmhouse

2 Talk about the types of housing that are common in your country.
   Most people live in ... Some people ... A few people ...

LISTENING

3 🔊 **Listen to a man describing one of the pictures.**

1 Which picture is he describing?

2 In which order does he describe the following parts of the picture?
   a) the background
   b) the foreground

3 In which order does he describe:
   a) the physical setting?
   b) the building?
   c) other details?
   Why do you think he describes them in this order?

WRITING

5 Stay in your groups. Use words and phrases from Exercise 4 to complete this description of one of the other pictures.

In the foreground, a woman and child are sitting on the balcony of their flat. They're wearing ^{1}..... clothes, and they're ^{2}..... quite poor. ^{3}..... their flat, the council's building a new road – or ^{4}..... it's a bridge. The side of the bridge is very ^{5}..... to the flat and there's a worker on a ladder only a few metres away. A second man is standing ^{6}..... the bridge, and he's working too. ^{7}..... him, on another balcony, a child is looking down. In the background there are some hills. ^{8}..... the new bridge and the hills are a number of white ^{9}..... houses with ^{10}..... red roofs.

SPEAKING

6 Look at the picture at the top of this page. What can you imagine about the lifestyles of the people who live there? Discuss:

a) what they do inside their home
b) what they eat and drink
c) the kind of work they do
d) what they do when they are not working

7 Work in pairs.
Student A: Imagine that you are standing at a distance from the building where you live, looking at the building and at the surrounding area from one particular position. Describe to your partner the picture that you see in your mind.
Student B: Draw the picture that your partner describes. Ask questions if you are not sure about something. When your partner has finished, ask questions about the lifestyles of the people inside and make notes.

Then change roles.

8 Use your drawing and your notes to describe your partner's home to the class.

Language reference

1 Used to

USES

Used to refers to:

- repeated events in the past, to stress how regular or frequent an event was in the past and to contrast that with the present.
  EXAMPLE: I **used to** swim a lot, but now I just don't have the time.

- continuous situations in the past, often to contrast a past with a present situation.
  EXAMPLES: She **used to** work in advertising, but she gave it up. There **used to** be green fields here, but now there's a shopping centre.

We can always use the past simple instead of used to, but used to emphasises one of the meanings above. We cannot always use used to instead of the past simple.

FORMS

- Used to is followed by an infinitive.
  EXAMPLE: I used to **enjoy** my work.

- We form the negative and question in the same way as regular verbs.
  EXAMPLES: How much **did** they **use to** read? They **didn't use to** read much. (or, more common: They **never used to** read much.)

2 Present simple

USES

The present simple is used to talk about:

- present habits or routines. It is often used with adverbs of frequency.
  EXAMPLE: She **often plays** tennis at weekends.

- present situations that continue for a long time.
  EXAMPLE: She **lives** in Cambridge.

FORMS

- Affirmative forms are the same as the infinitive without to, except that we add an s with he, she and it.
  EXAMPLES: I **work** here. She **works** here.

- We form the negative and question with do/does (not) + infinitive.
  EXAMPLES: **Do** you **live** here? He **doesn't** often **come**.

3 Adverbs of frequency

USE

- We use adverbs of frequency to say how often something happens.
  EXAMPLE: They **often** visit Britain.

POSITION

- Adverbs of frequency usually come before the main verb or after the verb to be.
  EXAMPLES: We **sometimes** eat out. They are **hardly ever** here.
  They come after auxiliary and modal verbs.
  EXAMPLE: I can **usually** leave early.

- Sometimes and occasionally can also come at the beginning or end of a sentence. We can also put usually and often at the beginning of a sentence.
  EXAMPLES: I sleep all weekend **sometimes**. **Usually** we go for a run before school.

- Other expressions of frequency, such as once a week, twice a month, three times a year, usually occur at the end of a sentence.

4 Present progressive

USES

The present progressive is used to talk about:

- present and temporary activities.
  EXAMPLE: Where's Susan? She's **working** at home today.

- fixed future plans, often with a future time adverbial.
  EXAMPLE: When **are** you **going** on holiday? We're **going** next Tuesday.

FORMS

- The form of the present progressive is to be + present participle (-ing form).
  EXAMPLES: They're **playing** outside. I'm not **leaving** until next week. Why **are** you **crying**?

FUNCTIONAL LANGUAGE

1 Greeting people
Hi!/Hello.
Good morning/afternoon/evening.

2 Talking about health
How are you?
Fine, thanks. And you?

3 Introducing people
Jane, this is Tim.
Jane, let me introduce you to Tim Reeves.

4 Responding to introductions
Nice to meet you.
Pleased to meet you.
How do you do?

5 Describing location/people/buildings
She's sitting in front of her house.
She's wearing casual clothes.
The house is painted blue.

Progress check Unit 1

GRAMMAR AND FUNCTIONS

1 Complete the questions with *used to* + infinitive or a present simple verb form.

BEFORE MARRIAGE

Sheila language student
small flat   discos, clubs
holidays abroad

Tim philosophy student
student hostel   films, concerts
cycling holidays

AFTER MARRIAGE

teachers
houseboat
parties
cruises on the boat

1 Who . . . . . languages? Sheila did.
2 What . . . . . she . . . . . now? She's a teacher.
3 Where . . . . . Tim . . . . . ? In a hostel.
4 Where . . . . . he and Sheila . . . . . now? On a houseboat.
5 . . . . . they . . . . . to discos? No, they don't.
6 What . . . . . they . . . . . in the evenings? They go to parties.
7 . . . . . Tim . . . . . to parties? No, he didn't.
8 Where . . . . . Sheila . . . . . on holiday? Abroad.
9 . . . . . she . . . . . abroad these days? No, she doesn't.
10 . . . . . they . . . . . on holiday together? No, they didn't.

2 Correct these statements about Sheila and Tim.

Tim used to study languages.
He didn't use to study languages. He used to study philosophy.

1 Sheila used to go to concerts.
2 Sheila and Tim live in a flat.
3 They work in an office.
4 They used to go on walking holidays.
5 Tim goes to concerts.

3 In which of these sentences can you replace the past simple form with *used to*? Rewrite those sentences.

1 Sheila studied Arabic and Persian.
2 She took her final exams last year.
3 Tim cycled with friends at weekends.
4 He went to concerts once or twice a week.
5 They bought their houseboat when they got married.

4 Reorder the prompts to make statements using present simple or present progressive forms of the verbs.

1 his/visit/weekend/they/parents/next
2 parties/often/on/give/boat/they/the
3 teach/the/Sheila/moment/at
4 this/not/morning/Tim/work
5 go/weekdays/ever/they/on/hardly/out

5 Complete the dialogues.

BARRY: ¹ . . . . . , Tim! How are you?
TIM: ² . . . . . . ³ . . . . . ?
BARRY: Oh, not so bad. Tim, ⁴ . . . . . Sue. She lives on the houseboat over there.
TIM: ⁵ . . . . . , Sue.
SUE: And you. Are you enjoying life on the river?

MS BAINES: ⁶ . . . . . , Mrs Fleetwood.
SHEILA: Good morning, Ms Baines.
MS BAINES: ⁷ . . . . Mr Stanley. He's a school governor. Mr Stanley, Mrs Fleetwood is one of our newest teachers.
MR STANLEY: ⁸ . . . . . , Mrs Fleetwood?
SHEILA: ⁹ . . . . . ?

VOCABULARY

6 Make seven compound nouns by using a word from each list.

LIST A
house   life   street   film   community
river   insurance

LIST B
company   boat   show   style   spirit
market   bus

15

2 Pleasures

An evening at home

Focus

TOPIC
- Television viewing

GRAMMAR
- Adjective + preposition + noun/-ing
- Love, like, enjoy, hate, prefer + -ing

FUNCTIONS
- Stating preferences

SKILLS
- Reading: an article

GETTING STARTED

1 Discuss your television viewing habits.

1 Is there a television in your house? If not, why not? If there is one, how many hours do you watch it on a typical evening?
2 What programmes do you watch? Why?
3 Do you think watching television is good for both children and adults?

READING

2 Read the introductory paragraph of the article on the right.

1 Describe the experiment. What did each family have to do?
2 What do you think happened?

3 Now read the rest of the article and complete the chart.

	BEFORE THE EXPERIMENT	DURING THE EXPERIMENT
George	ate in front of the TV	ate/talked with the family
Sandra	.....	.....
Angela	.....	.....
Peter	.....	.....

4 Find words in the article that mean:

1 a television (*n, informal*)
2 to hurry (*v*)
3 to feel unhappy about something that isn't there (*v*)
4 mad (*adj*)
5 to try to persuade someone by complaining a lot (*v*)
6 very sad (*adj*)

Don't take our box away!
by Sophie Barnes

The Carter family are television addicts and can't imagine life without one. The Fox family have never had a TV. We asked these two families to take part in an experiment. We took the Carters' television away from them for a month and gave it to the Fox family. This was the result.

■ *The Carter Family* ■

George Carter (father): At first, we all went into the living room as usual, but we didn't know what to do. All the chairs in the room have always faced the TV. In the first week we kept talking about the programmes we couldn't see, but after about ten days we started to think of ways of filling our time. We sat down together for meals instead of eating in front of the box; we talked to each other, because nobody had to rush away to see a programme. I do miss my favourite programmes, though. I prefer having a TV, but perhaps we can try to control how much we watch in future.

Sandra Carter (daughter, 15): I love watching TV. We've got satellite TV and I used to watch MTV all evening. I thought Mum and Dad were crazy to take part in this experiment. It was difficult at school because everyone talks about what they saw on TV the night before. But we did start to play games together – chess, cards, board games. We were more relaxed as a family. I had more time to do my homework and I even started taking piano lessons. Actually, I think I'd rather not have a TV for the next few months. If it's there, I watch it, and I've got my exams in two months' time.

■ The Fox Family ■

Angela Fox (mother): I have never wanted a television in my house. I think they're bad for children. When the TV arrived, we decided to put it in a little room at the top of the house so that we actually had to *choose* to watch it. We limited the children to two hours a day, but it was still too much. We hardly ever saw them, and they were never satisfied with the two hours. I watched a few films, and I was interested in some news and documentary programmes, but I hated planning our lives around the TV. We only ate together when nobody wanted to watch it! For the first time I had to nag the kids to do their homework. I didn't enjoy having a TV here. In fact I'd rather live in a house without TV or radio – all you hear is depressing news!

Peter Fox (son, 13): It was great! I liked having a TV. The only problem was that my sister and I never wanted to watch the same programmes, but you get bored with playing family games and reading and I was tired of doing the same things every day. The TV didn't affect my schoolwork badly – actually, there were lots of programmes that helped me with it.

DISCOVERING LANGUAGE

5 Find these adjectives in the article:
interested   bored   tired

1 Which preposition follows each adjective?
2 Which of these constructions can follow the preposition?
   a) a noun   b) an *-ing* verb form
   c) an infinitive
3 Find examples of these verbs in the article:
   love   like   enjoy   hate
   Which construction often follows them?

6 Make a list of at least ten things you can do at home in the evening (*play computer games, play board games ...*). Then interview your partner about what he/she likes doing at home in the evening, and what he/she gets bored with.

Do you enjoy ... ? Are you interested in ... ?

Now write sentences about your partner.

She's bored with/tired of watching television, but she doesn't enjoy playing board games either.

FOCUS ON FUNCTIONS

7 Look at this dialogue. The expressions in *italics* are from the article.

A Shall we go out for a meal on Thursday?

B 1 *I prefer* staying at home during the week.
   2 *I'd rather not.* Friday's a busy day.
   3 *I'd rather* eat at home.

1 Which of B's responses state(s):
   a) a specific preference?   b) a general preference?
2 Which constructions follow the expressions in italics?
3 What is the full form of *'d*?
4 How would you make Sentence 3 negative?
5 Which single word can replace *all* of B's responses?
6 So what is an important reason for using the expressions in italics?

8 Work in pairs.

Student A: Suggest an activity for this evening. If B refuses, try other evenings/activities.

Student B: Refuse A's suggestions politely. Make an excuse or state your own preference. Accept only after at least four suggestions. Then change roles.

Would you like to see a film tonight?

I'd rather not. I've got to... wash my hair.

A

B

Focus

TOPIC
• A visit to a film studio

GRAMMAR
• *So do I.*
• *Neither/Nor do I.*

FUNCTIONS
• Agreeing and disagreeing

SKILLS
• Reading: texts from a brochure
• Listening: sound sequences, a conversation
• Speaking: agreeing and disagreeing in conversation

Welcome to UNIVERSAL STUDIOS Florida, USA!

As a guest of Universal Studios Florida, the largest working film and television production studio outside Hollywood, you discover the secrets of how we make movie magic.

A day out

GETTING STARTED

1 Read the brochure and answer the questions.

1 Where is Universal Studios?
2 What do they produce there?
3 Where else in the USA are there similar studios?
4 Can visitors:
   a) go on rides?
   b) visit famous places?
   c) see where films are made?
   d) meet actors?
   e) make films?
5 Some people think this kind of entertainment is a waste of money. What do you think?

SPEAKING

2 Look at Pictures A – C. Which rides do you think the scenes are from? Why do you think so?

READING

3 Now read these descriptions of the attractions above.

1 Match the descriptions with the pictures and with these titles:
   Kongfrontation®   Ghostbusters™
   Earthquake®... The Big One
2 Where are the visitors to the *Earthquake*®... *The Big One* and *Kongfrontation*® rides? What imaginary danger are they in?

1 He weighs 13,000 pounds and he's angry! He's going crazy in New York, smashing skyscrapers and crushing cars – and he's got his giant eye on *you*! He's so close you can smell his hot banana breath and he's got you where he wants you – trapped in a tram high above the East River. But today's your lucky day. You survive to tell the story and you even see a video of your incredible experience!

2 Your worst nightmare has come true! You're in San Francisco when the big earthquake hits – and you're hopelessly trapped in an underground train while the world collapses around you. Will you be buried alive, or will it be the runaway train, the burning oil tanker or the huge wave that finally finishes you off?

3 The famous *Ghostbusters*™ team from Columbia Pictures is back on the New York streets fighting the evil Gozer and an assortment of ghosts with their high-tech guns. Watch out for the Marshmallow Man!

C

See the fantastic movie sets, meet film stars and terrifying monsters, and experience rides that take you into some of the most exciting films ever made. Fantasy becomes reality as you feel, see, hear, touch, smell, taste and live the ultimate in entertainment!

4 Find the adjectives in List A in the texts. Then match a word from List A with a word or a phrase with a similar meaning from List B.

LIST A
fantastic   terrifying   crazy   incredible   huge   famous   evil

LIST B
well-known   great   unbelievable   enormous   bad and dangerous   very frightening   wild

5 Now find verbs in the texts that mean:

1 breaking violently
2 breaking something by pressing it hard
3 caught so that you cannot escape
4 continue living after a dangerous experience
5 falls down
6 completely covered, usually underground

🖼 Documentary

LISTENING

6 Before you listen, work in pairs and make a list of the sounds that visitors to the studio might hear at each attraction.
Kongfrontation® : the sound of King Kong roaring

7 🔊 Listen to three sets of sounds from the attractions at Universal Studios, Florida.

1 Match what you hear to the texts and the pictures.
2 Make notes on what you hear.
   People are screaming and shouting.

8 Which of the attractions would you enjoy most? Why? Are there any that you wouldn't enjoy? Why not?

9 🔊 Listen to two people who have just visited one of the attractions.

1 Which attraction was it? Did they both like everything about it?
2 Write the expressions that follow these comments.
   I was terrified!   *So was I!*
   a) I don't know how they do it.
   b) I didn't like the water.
   c) I'm really thirsty.
   d) I'm not interested in food at the moment.

DISCOVERING LANGUAGE

10 Look at the responses you gave in Exercise 9, question 2.

1 Which of the responses are used to agree with:
   a) an affirmative statement?
   b) a negative statement?
2 Which response shows that the second speaker disagrees?
3 Which comes first, the subject or the verb, when the second speaker:
   a) agrees?   b) disagrees?
4 What do you notice about the verb form in the comment and the verb form in the response?

SPEAKING

11 Work in pairs.

Student A: Tell your partner where you were born, your age, if you are married, something you enjoy, something you do not enjoy, what you did yesterday evening.

Student B: Respond to Student A, using *So ...*, *Neither ...*, *Nor ...* or a phrase like *I was(n't)*.

Then change roles.

CREATIVE WRITING

Describing scenes

Focus

TOPIC
- Landscapes

SKILLS
- Speaking: description of sensations
- Reading: a literary extract
- Writing: a description of a scene, making comparisons

VOCABULARY DEVELOPMENT
- Adjectives associated with colour words
- Verbs referring to light

SPEAKING

1 Imagine you are the person in the picture. It is the end of a beautiful summer day. It is beginning to get dark and everything is very peaceful.

1 Think of nouns for things that you can see. *sky, hill* …
2 Think of adjectives that you can use to describe what you can see. *blue* (sky), *steep* (hill) …
3 The picture gives us only a visual image. Close your eyes and imagine what else you are experiencing. How do you feel? What can you hear, smell and taste?
4 Compare what you hear, smell and taste with your partner.

READING: A LITERARY EXTRACT

2 The extract on the right comes from *Neither Here Nor There* by Bill Bryson, an American travel writer. In the extract the author is standing on a hill on the island of Capri, off the coast of southern Italy. Read and answer the questions.

1 What time of day is it?
2 How high is he above the sea?
3 How windy is it on the hill?
4 Are there any plants on the hillside?

3 Think about these questions and discuss them. Justify your answers.

1 Does the writer live near Capri?
2 Is he alone on the platform?
3 Can he see the sun?
4 What is Sainsbury's?
5 Do you think the author has a sense of humour?

4 Find words in the text that mean:

1 vertical
2 a blue-green colour
3 rough and uneven with sharp points
4 quietest
5 a very thin piece
6 a sweet-smelling climbing plant

5 Work in pairs and find words and phrases that help to create a picture of what the writer can:

a) see   b) hear   c) smell   d) feel

---

20   NEITHER HERE NOR THERE

It was nearly dusk. A couple of hundred yards further on the path rounded a bend through the trees and ended suddenly, breathtakingly, in a viewing platform hanging out over a rock face – like a little patio in the sky. It was a look-out built for the public, but I had the feeling that no one had been there for years, certainly no tourist.

I have never seen anything half as beautiful: on one side the town of Capri spilling down the hillside, on the other the twinkling lights of the cove at Anacapri and the houses gathered around it, and in front of me a sheer drop of – what? – 200 feet,

DEVELOPING VOCABULARY

6 Think about different ways of describing colour.

1 Which of these colour expressions have similar meanings?

deep blue   pale blue   brilliant blue
bright blue   light blue   dark blue

2 Now look at these colour expressions, which start with nouns instead of adjectives:

rose pink   sea green   jet black   mud brown
blood red

   a) What does each expression mean? Check new words in your dictionary.

   b) How do you express these meanings in your language?

   c) Try to make other colour expressions in English.   *ink black, coal black*

7 The verbs below are all related to light. Use a dictionary to match them with nouns that they commonly describe.

VERBS
flash   flicker   twinkle   shine   sparkle
NOUNS
the sun   diamonds   lightning   stars   candles

NEITHER HERE NOR THERE   21

300 feet, to a sea of the deepest aquamarine washing against the jagged rocks. The sea was so far below that the sound of breaking waves reached me as the faintest of whispers. A sliver of moon, brilliantly white, hung in a pale blue evening sky, a warm breeze pulled gently at my hair and everywhere there was the scent of lemon, honeysuckle and pine. It was like being in the household products section of Sainsbury's. Ahead of me there was nothing but open sea, calm and seductive, for 150 miles to Sicily.

~

8 Look at the picture below and write sentences about it, using the same constructions as Bill Bryson.

1 *The sea was **so far below that** …*
   The sky seemed so close that I felt I could touch it.

2 ***It was like** be**ing** in the household products section of Sainsbury's.*
   It was like standing on top of the world.

WRITING

9 Liz and Elsa visited Nepal on holiday. Read about their experience of watching the sun rise over the Himalayas. Then work with a partner and continue the account, using information in the picture and your imagination. Describe what you saw, heard, smelt and felt. Use the expressions in Exercises 6–8 to help you.

❝We were in Nepal and it was spring. We wanted to see the sun rise over Annapurna, one of the highest mountains in the Himalayas. We spent the night in a small hotel at the bottom of Poon Hill. In the morning we woke up at four a.m. and climbed in the dark, through the trees, to the top. We were wearing thick sweaters and heavy boots. It was cold. The top of Poon Hill is about 4,000 metres above sea level. We sat down, had breakfast in the dark, and waited for dawn.

Then the sun rose, … ❞

10 Read your text again. Ask yourselves questions and make improvements.

1 Have you described the effects on all your senses?
2 Can you improve the vocabulary you have used?
3 Have you used structures from Exercise 8?
4 Have you made any grammatical or spelling errors?
5 Have you used appropriate punctuation?

11 Write about a similar experience that you have had.

Language reference

1 Adjectives followed by particular prepositions: *interested, bored, tired*

- These adjectives can all be used alone.
  EXAMPLE: *I'm tired.*
- When we want to give more information after the adjective, we can use a preposition: *interested in, bored with, tired of.* The preposition can be followed by an object (a noun phrase or a pronoun) or an *-ing* form.
  EXAMPLES: *Are you interested in **acting?** I'm bored with **my job**. He got tired of **her**.*

2 Verbs followed by *-ing/to* + infinitive/infinitive without *to*

USES
- The use of the *-ing* form after verbs such as *like, dislike, enjoy, hate* and *prefer* suggests that we actually do the activity or have done it.
  EXAMPLES: *I **don't like** playing squash. I **prefer** jogging.*
- *I'd like ...* refers to something that we want to do. It may be possible or impossible.
  EXAMPLE: *I'd like to dance on the moon.*
- *I'd rather ...* is used to express preferences when we consider alternatives or contrast our own views with another person's views.
  EXAMPLE: *'It's such a lovely day. Let's go out.' 'I'd rather stay in and watch the football on TV.'*

FORMS
- Verbs of liking, disliking and preference are often followed by an *-ing* form.
  EXAMPLE: *I **enjoy jogging**.*
- *I'd like ...* is followed by an infinitive with *to*.
  EXAMPLE: *I'd like to see you.*
- *I'd rather ...* is followed by an infinitive without *to*.
  EXAMPLE: *I'd rather see a film than a play.*

3 *So, neither* and *nor*

USES
- We use *So ...* to agree with a speaker who has made an affirmative statement.
  EXAMPLE: *'We love animals.' 'So do we.'*
- We use *Neither ...* or *Nor ...* to agree with a speaker who has made a negative statement.
  EXAMPLE: *'I don't like travelling.' 'Neither/Nor do I.'*

FORMS
- The tense of the auxiliary verb in the response is the same as the tense of the verb in the original statement.
  EXAMPLE: *'She **hates** planes.' 'So **does** he.'*
- We change the order of the subject and the auxiliary verb to form the response.
  EXAMPLE: *'I **don't enjoy** American films.' 'Nor **do I**.'*

4 *So ... that*

- We use *so* + adjective + *that* to express strength of feeling about something or the degree of a certain quality that something has.
  EXAMPLES: *I was **so unhappy that** I had to talk to someone. The room was **so quiet that** you could hear a pin drop.*
- We can also use the structure *so* + adverb + *that*.
  EXAMPLE: *I walked **so far that** I had to catch a bus home.*

5 *Like* (preposition)

- *Like* is followed by a noun phrase or *-ing* form. It is used to make comparisons.
  EXAMPLES: *The beds were **like rocks**. Arriving at the top of the hill was **like coming** home.*

FUNCTIONAL LANGUAGE

1 Talking about a general preference
I prefer skiing (to riding).
I'd rather go riding than skiing in winter.

2 Talking about a specific preference
I'd rather play badminton this evening.

3 Agreeing with someone
We like children.   So do I.
They don't enjoy team games.   Nor do we.
Janet didn't go.   Neither did Bob.

4 Disagreeing with someone
I don't enjoy watching television.   I do!
I'm hungry.   I'm not!

5 Talking about degree
The view was so lovely that I cried.

6 Making comparisons
It was like leaving home forever.

Talkback

Working it out

What's your ideal job? Are you interested in earning a lot of money? Do you want to job-share and have time to bring up a family? Perhaps you want to help people in some way?

1 Look at the pictures. They each suggest a feature of a job that is important to some people. Which features are they? Make a list.

2 Can you think of any other features that people might find important in a job? Add them to your list.
   responsibility, promotion chances …

3 Now put all the features in order of their importance to you.

4 Show your list to your partner. Explain why you have chosen that order. Answer your partner's questions about your choice and say whether you agree/disagree with his/her choice.

5 Together think of jobs that you think match each of your lists.

6 Tell the class about the jobs you and your partner would like and explain why.

Lines on a map

Focus

TOPIC
• National borders

GRAMMAR
• *Have to, must, needn't*

FUNCTIONS
• Talking about obligation, absence of obligation, prohibition

SKILLS
• Listening: brief monologues
• Speaking: describing location
• Reading: an article

GETTING STARTED

1 Name the natural features in the pictures. Then match these countries to the features that form part of their borders.

1 the USA and Mexico   2 Chile and Argentina
3 Saudi Arabia and Oman

LISTENING

2 🖭 Listen to three people talking about the position of their countries.

1 Which country is each person from?
2 Which of the phrases on the right suggests that a feature is:
    a) outside the country?   *in the north*
    b) inside the country?   *to the south*
3 List the other compass directions that you hear.
    north, south ...

SPEAKING

3 Describe the position of your country and its borders. Then work in pairs.

Student A: Think of a country and describe its position to your partner.
Student B: Guess the country.

Then change roles.

READING

4 Look at the title of the article. What two meanings of *cross* does the writer intend? What do you think the article is about?

Borders that make people cross

5 Read the first paragraph and say how you think the article continues.

You have to have a passport if you want to go to another country, don't you? At least, that's what *Vitali Vitaliev* thought. But if it's Sunday, it seems you needn't worry ...

It sounds stupid to get lost in Liechtenstein, a country in the Alps so tiny that when you ask a local for directions to the post office, he'll probably say something like, 'Go to the next corner, turn right into Switzerland, cross the road back into Liechtenstein, and you'll see the post office at the next traffic lights, just opposite the Austrian border.'

6 Read the next part of the article. What happened to the writer? Why did he become so worried?

But after several hours of hiking through the Alps I did indeed get lost. So it was with some relief that I found myself walking down into a valley towards a country inn. The place was full of people, all with huge Wiener schnitzels on their plates, the area of some of them almost equal to that of Liechtenstein. Suddenly I froze: you find Wiener schnitzels of this size in only one country – Austria. I was now in Austria illegally!

Terrible visions from my Soviet past rushed at me. Words like 'extradition', 'deportation' and 'detention' started echoing in my brain. With alarm I remembered that my brand-new Australian passport was in my hotel in Liechtenstein. And it didn't have an Austrian visa anyway!

Like any former Soviet citizen, I have a deeply rooted fear of borders. Even now, with a western passport in my pocket, I find it hard to get used to immigration officials at western airports waving me through. I am scared that they might forget to put some important stamp in my passport, and this will mean trouble. I linger in front of an immigration officer with a sycophantic look on my face. I know I mustn't look too confident. Old habits die hard. Old fears die even harder.

I had to do something – quickly. I rushed out of the Austrian inn and went back down the road towards the Liechtenstein border. In the distance I could see the tiny hut of a border post and I prepared myself for a painful showdown with the frontier guards.

7 What do you think happened next? Discuss possible endings, and then turn to page 31 to find out what really happened.

8 Consider these questions about the article.

1 Where did the writer use to live?
2 What passport has he got now?
3 Where did he leave his passport?
4 What did he do when he realised that he was in Austria?
5 Why do you think former Soviet citizens might have a fear of borders?
6 Why does the writer not want to look too confident at borders?
7 Why does he believe there will be a 'painful showdown'?

9 Complete the text with these words:

visas   passports   stamps   border post   frontier guards   immigration office

We arrived at the small [1]...... Two [2]..... stopped us and pointed to the window of the [3]..... . A woman took our [4]..... and looked carefully at our [5]..... . Then she put the entry [6]..... in our passports and returned them.

Use the context to guess the meaning of other new words in the article. Then check with your dictionary.

DISCOVERING LANGUAGE

10 Look at these sentences and answer the questions.

A *You* **have to** *have a passport.*
B *You* **don't have to** *have a passport.*
C *I* **had to** *do something – quickly.*
D *I* **didn't have to** *do it.*
E *If it's Sunday, you* **needn't** *worry.*
F *You* **don't need to** *worry.*
G *I know I* **mustn't** *look too confident.*

1 What part of speech follows the verbs in **bold** type?
2 What are the negative forms of *have to* and *must?* What is special about the negative of *need?*
3 Choose a verb from A–G above to replace the words in **bold**.

H *I* **must** *get to the station by five o'clock.*
I *You* **don't have to** *pay for children.*

4 Now rewrite these two sentences in the past.

FOCUS ON FUNCTIONS

11 Match these functions to sentences A–I in Exercise 10.

a) obligation   b) absence of obligation   c) prohibition

12 Look at the signs below and write sentences using verbs from Exercise 10 with the words below each sign.

British passport holders do not require a visa for the USA	It is forbidden to take Latvian currency out of the country	We only accept American Express cheques	Please walk on the right	BOARDING .... First class passengers only ....
1 (have)	2 (take)	3 (pay with)	4 (walk)	5 (wait)

Coming and going

Focus

TOPICS
- Air travel
- Customs

GRAMMAR
- Reported requests and orders

SKILLS
- Listening: extracts from conversations, conversations at customs
- Speaking: discussion, role play

SPEECH PATTERNS
- Stress and intonation of orders and requests

GETTING STARTED

1 Look at the cartoon.

1 What comment do you think the cartoonist is making?
2 Has anyone ever searched your luggage? What did they tell you to do? Did they ask you any questions?
3 Do you think there's too much security at airports? Why (not)?

LISTENING

2 Before you listen, look at this list of jobs connected with travel.

passport officer   flight attendant   porter
pilot   customs officer   check-in clerk
security guard

Which person:

a) searches your baggage before you travel?
b) checks your baggage when you enter a country?
c) examines your travel documents when you enter or leave a country?
d) serves you food and drink?
e) checks your plane ticket before you travel?
f) carries your bags?
g) flies the plane?

3 ▭ Listen to some extracts from conversations on a plane and at an airport. Match them with the people in Exercise 2.

4 ▭ Listen again. Is each of these extracts: a) an order?   b) a polite request?

DISCOVERING LANGUAGE

5 Study these two dialogues and answer the questions.

1 ATTENDANT: Please don't smoke here.
   A: What did he say?
   B: He told us not to smoke here.
2 ATTENDANT: Could you fasten your seat belts?
   A: What did she say?
   B: She asked us to fasten our seat belts.

1 In each dialogue, is the attendant:
   a) asking a real question?
   b) making a statement?
   c) making a request?
   d) giving an order?
2 Which verbs does B use to report these two functions?
3 What part of speech follows immediately after the reporting verb?
4 What is the form of the verb that is reported?
5 Can you think of another, stronger verb for reporting orders?

6 Work in groups of three.

Student A: Read aloud the sentences below.
Student B: Ask Student C what A said.
Student C: Report what A said using *ask, tell* or *order.*
A: Can you close the window, please?
B: *What did he say?*
C: *He asked you to close the window.*

1 Put your seat belt on, please.
2 Fill in the form.
3 Could you bring me a glass of water?
4 Don't put bags under the seats.
5 Would you open the case, please?
6 Stand over there.

▣ Documentary

LISTENING

7 Before you listen, look at the pictures.

1 Who are the people?
2 Where are they?
3 Which country are they in?
4 What questions do you think the man in uniform is asking?
5 What is the purpose of the form?

WELCOME TO THE UNITED STATES

DEPARTMENT OF THE TREASURY
UNITED STATES CUSTOMS SERVICE   FORM APPROVED OMB NO. 1515-0041

CUSTOMS DECLARATION

Each arriving traveler or head of family must provide the following information (only **ONE** written declaration per family is required):

1. Name: ....
   Last   _First_   _Middle Initial_

2. Date of Birth: ...../...../.....   3. Airline/Flight ....
   Day Month Year

4. Number of family members traveling with you ....

5. U.S. Address: ....
   City: .... State: ....

6. I am a U.S. Citizen   YES NO
   If No,   ☐   ☐
   Country: ....

7. I reside permanently in the U.S.   YES NO
   If No,   ☐   ☐
   Expected Length of Stay: ....

8. The purpose of my trip is or was ☐ BUSINESS ☐ PLEASURE

9. I am/we are bringing fruits, plants, meats, food,   YES NO
   soil, birds, snails, other live animals, farm   ☐   ☐
   products, or I/we have been on a farm or ranch
   outside the U.S.

10. I am/we are carrying currency or monetary   YES NO
    instruments over $10,000 U.S. or foreign   ☐   ☐
    equivalent.

11. The total value of all goods I/we purchased or
    acquired abroad and am/are bringing to the U.S.
    is (see instructions under Merchandise on reverse
    side): $ ....
                                      US Dollars

▶ **MOST MAJOR CREDIT CARDS ACCEPTED.**
SIGN ON REVERSE SIDE AFTER YOU READ WARNING.
(Do not write below this line.)

INSPECTOR'S NAME   STAMP AREA

BADGE NO.

Paperwork Reduction Act Notice: The Paperwork Reduction Act of 1980 says we must tell you why we are collecting this information, how we will use it and whether you have to give it to us. We ask for this information to carry out the Customs, Agriculture, and Currency laws of the United States. We need it to ensure that travelers are complying with these laws and to allow us to figure and collect the right amount of duties and taxes. Your response is mandatory.

Customs Form 6059B (042988)

8 Study the form and find sentences or phrases that mean:

1 I have a US passport
2 I live in the United States
3 money in cash or document form
4 things that I bought
5 things we got in another country
6 on the back (of the form)

9 ▭ James P McKenna and his daughter Carrie live in Chicago in the USA. They have just returned from a holiday in Europe on Flight AA460. Listen and complete the declaration form with their details.

10 ▭ Listen to a second conversation and answer these questions.

1 What gifts is the traveller bringing into the US?
2 Which does the officer look at?
3 Where did she buy the perfume?
4 How much did she pay for it?
5 Why will the traveller have to put the perfume in her declaration?

SPEECH PATTERNS

11 ▭ Listen to the same sentence said in two different ways.

Could you open your bag, please?

1 Which is said as a) a request?   b) an order?
2 Does the voice go up or down at the end of the request?
3 Listen and repeat each sentence.
4 Now say this sentence in two different ways: _Could you wait there?_

SPEAKING

12 Work in pairs.

Student A: You are a customs officer. Your partner is a tourist visiting the USA. Inside his/her case are four parcels. You need to know what is in each one, if they are gifts or for personal use, and how much each gift cost. Ask Student B to open two of the parcels.

Student B: Turn to page 128.

> A
>
> Tues. 24/6
>
> Jenny,
> Having a fantastic time. Staying
> on a campsite near a huge sandy
> beach. Plenty of nightlife, and the
> weather's great! Went
> hang-gliding yesterday. Some
> people took us to a hill a few
> miles away. Terrifying, but I'm still
> alive - just! Hiring some bikes
> tomorrow to explore the island.
> Best wishes,
> Sarah
>
> Ms J Price
> 10 Lake Crescent
> Glasgow
> G42 7FY

Focus

TOPIC
• Holiday postcards

SKILLS
• Reading: postcards
• Writing: a postcard

VOCABULARY DEVELOPMENT
• Adjectives describing places, feelings and experiences
• Adjectives ending in -ed/-ing

Sending postcards

🔄 COMPARING CULTURES

1 This page shows how British people write postcards. Think about postcards that you write or receive.

1 Do you send picture postcards? If so, how often do you write them and who do you send them to?
2 Why do people send picture postcards? What is their general purpose?
3 What kind of information do people in your country usually include on a holiday postcard? Compare this with the postcards above.

READING

2 Read the postcards and answer these questions. Give reasons for your answers.

1 Which of the writers do you think is on holiday abroad?
2 What is the relationship between:
   a) Jenny and Sarah? b) Ken and Julie?
3 Which of the endings below are possible alternatives for:
   a) both postcards?
   b) neither postcard?
   c) Sarah's postcard only?
   d) Julie's postcard only?

   Regards   Love   Take care
   Yours faithfully   Yours sincerely

3 Look at the postcards again.

1 Holiday postcards are often very similar. Which of these features do the writers of both postcards include?
   a) descriptions of general feelings about the holiday
   b) comments about the weather
   c) feelings about the person they are writing to
   d) descriptions of where they are staying
   e) what they plan to do
   f) recommendations
   g) what they did yesterday
   h) closing words
2 What do you think XXXX means at the bottom of postcard B?
3 What features of the style of Postcard A are acceptable in postcards but not in formal letters? Change Postcard B so that the style is the same.

B Dear Ken
I arrived last night after an awful flight – there were long delays at the airport. The hotel's very noisy and the food's really disgusting. I'm having a rotten time and I miss you a lot! At least the weather's not too bad. I'm going down to the coast later today to try to find a quiet beach. I can't wait to see you again.
        All my love,
        Julie ××××

Ken Ellis
27 Thirsk Road
Norwich
NR5 IPX
England UK

DEVELOPING VOCABULARY

4 Look again at Postcard A.

1 Which adjectives does Sarah use to complete these sentences?
Having a(n) ¹..... time.
Staying on a campsite near a(n) ²..... ³..... beach.
The weather's ⁴..... .

2 Which of these adjectives could you put in the gaps above?
1 *amazing, dreadful, awful, ...*
amazing dreadful small awful beautiful stony miserable empty long wonderful OK nice good not bad tiny sheltered marvellous exciting lovely appalling superb immense rocky fine enormous crowded tolerable

3 Which adjectives express positive feelings? Which ones express negative feelings? Can you think of other words that could fit the sentences?

5 Look at these sentences describing experiences:

A *It was terrifying.*
B *The food's disgusting.*

1 How did the person feel in each case?

2 Which of these adjectives refer to experiences? Which refer to people's feelings?
bored interested disappointed exciting amazed appalling frightening relaxed surprised depressed

3 Complete these sentences with the correct form of the word in brackets.
a) We're the only guests in the hotel. It's very ..... (depress)
b) I'm going skiing tomorrow. I'm really ..... (excite)
c) Meals are cheap. We're quite ..... (surprise)
d) There was a small earthquake yesterday. It was ..... (frighten)
e) We visited some ..... places yesterday. (interest)

WRITING

6 Work with a partner. Choose one of the postcards on these pages and imagine that you are on holiday there.

1 How do you feel about this place? Are you having a good time? Make a list of words and phrases that you can use to describe the place and your feelings about it.

2 Think of an English-speaking person that you would like to write to. How well do you know him/her? What is an appropriate way to end your postcard?

3 Decide what you did yesterday. Where did you go? How did you get there? What was it like? How did you feel?

4 Imagine something you plan to do tomorrow.

7 Write your postcard together. Follow this sequence:

1 Dear ...
2 your general feelings about the holiday
3 the place where you are staying
4 the weather
5 what you did yesterday
6 what you plan to do tomorrow
7 ending

Language reference

GRAMMAR

1 *Have to*, *must* and *needn't*

USES

- We use affirmative and question forms of *must* and *have to* to express obligation.
  EXAMPLES: *We **must** wait here. **Do** I **have to** go?*
- We use *must not/mustn't* to express prohibition.
  EXAMPLE: *You **mustn't** be late.*
- We use *need not/needn't* and *do/does not have to* to say that there is no obligation to do something.
  EXAMPLE: *You **needn't/don't have to** come if you're busy.*

FORMS

- *Have to*, *must* and *needn't* are followed by the infinitive of another verb without *to*.
  EXAMPLES: *He **has to fill in** a form. He **must do** it now. He **needn't complete** the last section.*
- We make negative forms and questions in the following ways:
  Have to: We use *do not/don't* or *does not/doesn't*.
  EXAMPLES: *We **don't have to** go yet. **Do** you **have to** go?*
  Must: We add *not/n't* for the negative.
  EXAMPLE: *They **mustn't** start before eight o'clock.*
  We reverse the order of the subject and *must* to form questions.
  EXAMPLE: ***Must we** pay extra?*
  Need: We add *not/n't* for the negative.
  EXAMPLE: *You **needn't** ask her permission.*
  Do (not/n't) or *does (not/n't)* are most commonly used in questions and are used as an alternative negative form. In these cases, *need* is followed by an infinitive with *to*.
  EXAMPLES: ***Do** I **need to** take a present? You **don't need to** ask her permission.*
- There is no past or *will* form of *must*. We use *had to* (past) and *will have to* (future).
  EXAMPLES: *We **had to** see her before she left. She'**ll have to** find somewhere to live when she gets there.*

2 Reported requests and orders

USES

- We can use *ask* to report requests and *tell* to report orders.
  EXAMPLES:
  Direct: 'Could you close the door?'
  Reported: *He **asked** me to close the door.*
  Direct: 'Close the door.'
  Reported: *He **told** me to close the door.*
- Other reporting verbs include: *beg* (for a desperate request), *order*, *instruct*, and *command* (for strong commands).

FORMS

- *Ask* and *tell* are followed by indirect object + *to* + infinitive. The indirect object is often an object pronoun.
  EXAMPLE: *I asked **her to help** me.*
- We report a negative request or command by putting *not* before *to* + infinitive.
  EXAMPLE:
  Direct: 'Please don't come back.'
  Reported: *He asked/told me **not** to come back.*
- Other changes may be necessary when a request or command is reported. These include:
  pronouns
  EXAMPLE: 'Can **you** help **me**?' → *He asked **me** to help **him**.*
  time/place adverbials
  EXAMPLES: 'Can you help me **this morning**?' → *He asked me to help him **that morning**. '*Leave your bags **here**.' → *She told me to leave my bags **there**.*
  particular verbs
  EXAMPLE: '**Bring** it to me.' → *She told me to **take** it to her.*

FUNCTIONAL LANGUAGE

1 Expressing obligation
We have to go to work now.
We must go to work now.

2 Expressing prohibition
You mustn't put your feet on the table.

3 Expressing lack of obligation
They needn't help us.
She doesn't need to be there.
I don't have to do any homework.

4 Reporting requests
I asked her to post the letter.

5 Reporting orders
He told me to open my suitcase.

Progress check Units 2–3

GRAMMAR AND FUNCTIONS

1 Reply to A's comments by agreeing. Use an expression beginning with *So* or *Neither/Nor*.

  A: I hate basketball.   B: *So do I.*

1 A: I didn't want to play.   B: . . . . .
2 A: I haven't got the right shoes. B: . . . . .
3 A: I was at the match yesterday. B: . . . . .
4 A: I'm bored with sport.   B: . . . . .
5 A: I can't go out tonight.   B: . . . . .

2 Report the requests and orders in *italics* in this dialogue. Start like this:

My mother told/asked . . .

MOTHER: ¹*Could you help me with the housework, please?*

SON: What do you want me to do?

MOTHER: ²*Can you clean the kitchen?* I'll do the bathroom.

SON: I'll do it later. I'm watching a video.

MOTHER: You can watch it later. ³*Turn the television off now.*

SON: In a minute . . .

MOTHER: ⁴*Don't talk to me like that!*

SON: What shall I do first?

MOTHER: ⁵*Could you do the washing-up?* ⁶*And please don't leave the saucepans for me!*

3 Read these sentences.

A We must arrive early.
B We don't have to arrive early.
C We needn't arrive early.
D We have to arrive early.

1 Which sentences have a similar meaning? Find two pairs.
2 Rewrite each sentence to refer to the past.

4 Reply to each question, using the prompts.

1 Shall we go to France this year? (I/rather/go/Ireland)
2 Why are you interested in Ireland? (I/enjoy/fish)
3 Do you think Ken wants to come with us? (Yes, he/probably/like/come)
4 We can go by train and boat, can't we? (I/prefer/drive/there)
5 Is it expensive to fly? (Ken/hate/fly)

VOCABULARY

5 Complete the dialogues with *-ing* or *-ed* forms of the verb in brackets.

1 A: Why were you . . . . . ?   (terrify)
   B: Flying is always . . . . . , don't you think?

2 A: I find flying extremely . . . . . .   (tire)
   B: Yes, I get . . . . . on long flights.

3 A: Airport security is . . . . . , isn't it? (annoy)
   B: Is it? I only feel . . . . . if I have to queue.

4 A: I'm never . . . . . in the departure lounge.   (relax)
   B: No, I agree. Waiting to board isn't . . . . . .

5 A: And foreign airports are particularly . . . . . .   (confuse)
   B: I know what you mean. I felt really . . . . . on my first visit to Nigeria.

. . . .

Unit 3: Lines on a map, Exercise 7

Now read the rest of the article. Did you guess the ending correctly?

A huge lock hung on the door of the empty border post. Above it was a sign: 'The frontier post is open daily from 8 a.m. to 8 p.m. except for holidays and weekends.' Remembering it was Sunday, I gave a sigh of relief and walked briskly across the border into Liechtenstein. No one was there to stop me.

4 Rights and wrongs

Bag snatchers!

Focus

TOPIC
- Crime

GRAMMAR
- Past progressive
- Past simple
- Conjunctions: *while/when*

SKILLS
- Reading: a report
- Listening: accounts of crimes
- Writing: a report
- Speaking: describing a crime

VOCABULARY DEVELOPMENT
- Words related to crime

GETTING STARTED

1 Look at the pictures below. Can you put them in the correct order? Describe what is happening, using present tenses to tell the story.

In the first picture, two boys are standing in a doorway. They're watching a woman who is waiting in the street.

READING

2 Read the report a witness wrote about the incident. Answer the questions.

1 Where was the witness at one o'clock?
2 Where were the boys?
3 Where was the woman?
4 What did she do?
5 What did the first boy do?
6 Then what did the other boy do?

> It was about one o'clock. I was sitting in a café on Queen Street when I noticed two boys, in their late teens, in a doorway opposite. They were watching a woman a few metres away from them. She was waiting in the street with her handbag under her arm and then, after a minute, she looked at her watch. While she was standing there, one of the boys snatched her bag. She turned quickly and shouted at him but he ran off down the street. While the thief was running away, the other boy started to walk away from the shop.

DISCOVERING LANGUAGE

3 Look back at the report above.

1 Find two different verb forms in the second sentence. Which one describes a situation in progress? Which one describes a sudden action?
2 Find other past progressive (*was/were + -ing*) and past simple forms. Why do you think the writer uses these tenses?
3 Which of the words *when* and *while* is commonly used to introduce a progressive verb form? Which is used to introduce a simple verb form?

4 Complete the dialogue between a police officer and the woman's husband.

OFFICER: What ..... you ..... (do) when your wife lost her bag?

MAN: I ..... (open) the car door.

OFFICER: ..... you ..... (watch) your wife?

MAN: No, I ..... . I ..... (face) the car.

5 Look at the pictures again. Make sentences about the different people.

While the man was unlocking his car, the thief snatched the woman's bag.

LISTENING

6 ▣ Listen to four people describing crimes. Match them with the pictures.

DEVELOPING VOCABULARY

7 ▣ Listen again.

1 Do these words from the interviews describe:
a) a person? b) a crime? c) something a criminal does?
shoplifting steal burglar burglary burgle rob
pickpocket thief theft vandalism arsonist mug murder

2 Write the words above and these words in the chart below. Use a dictionary to help you.
mugger robbery mugging vandal vandalise arson
murderer shoplifter robber murder

PERSON	SOMEONE WHO ...	NAME OF CRIME	ACTION VERB
burglar	takes things from houses	.....	.....
.....	takes things from pockets or bags	.X.	pick pockets
.....	damages other people's property	.....	.....
.....	burns other people's property	.....	set fire to
.....	attacks people outside for money	mugging	.....
.....	takes things from people/ buildings	robbery	.....
.....	takes other people's things (general)	.....	steal
.....	steals from shops	.....	steal
.....	kills people	.....	.....

SPEAKING

8 *Either:* **Choose a picture from Exercise 6 and make notes on what happened. Then work in pairs. Tell your partner your story and then listen to your partner's story. Ask questions for more information.**

Or: **Tell your partner about a crime you have witnessed or heard about.**

WRITING

9 **Write about the crime you described in Exercise 8. Use the report in Exercise 2 to help you.**

↻ COMPARING CULTURES

10 **In your country, what is the most common punishment for non-violent theft? Consider these possibilities. Are there any others?**

a) a warning   b) a short prison sentence   c) a long prison sentence
d) public embarrassment   e) community service   f) a fine

Focus

TOPIC
• Women police officers

GRAMMAR
• Reflexive pronouns

FUNCTIONS
• Agreeing and disagreeing with opinions

SKILLS
• Listening: a monologue, a narrative

Women in the front line

GETTING STARTED

1 What is happening in the pictures? What do you think the expression 'the front line' means?

FOCUS ON FUNCTIONS

2 Read the comments below about women police officers and discuss them with your partner. Which do you agree with? Which do you disagree with? What are your reasons?

AGREEING
I agree with (A) that …
I share (A)'s opinion.
I think (A) is absolutely right.

DISAGREEING
I don't agree with (A).
I disagree with (A).
It's wrong to say that …

A ❝ It's a mistake to send women into violent situations. There *is* a place for women in the police force – in *desk* jobs, not out on the streets where they're in danger. They can't look after themselves out there. ❞

B ❝ A woman police officer must think of herself as an officer first and a woman second. She has to do everything a man does or she can't expect to have a career in police work. ❞

C ❝ A man must protect himself. In difficult circumstances he hasn't got time to defend a female officer. It's wrong to expect that. ❞

D ❝ We need women officers out there in front of the public. Situations are less likely to become violent. Women know how to talk to people, to calm situations. People feel more threatened by male officers and this leads to confrontation. ❞

DISCOVERING LANGUAGE

3 Study these sentences from the comments.

A *They can't look after themselves out there.*
B *A woman police officer must think of herself …*
C *A man must protect himself.*

1 What is the object in each sentence?
2 When do we use *-self* and when do we use *-selves* in reflexive pronouns?
3 Consider these other examples. How is the reflexive pronoun formed? Identify the different patterns.
D *I've hurt myself.*
E *We controlled ourselves.*
F *Help yourself.*
G *Please behave yourselves.*
H *The dog protected itself.*

4 Use a reflexive pronoun to describe what each character below is doing.

🖼 Documentary

LISTENING

5 📼 Listen to Part 1 of an interview with Cathy Ellison, an American police officer from Austin, Texas. Choose the correct endings to these statements.

1 She has been a police officer for more than:
   a) 3 years   b) 13 years   c) 30 years
2 She investigates:
   a) murders   b) drug crimes   c) theft
3 After studying, new officers work:
   a) in an academy   b) in an office   c) on the streets
4 They have to:
   a) learn about a particular area   b) learn to drive
   c) learn a language
5 If a police officer is black rather than white, black people are:
   a) equally trusting   b) less trusting   c) more trusting
6 In a frightening situation it is important to:
   a) hide your feelings   b) show your feelings   c) leave the scene

6 Read the first part of Cathy's interview. Check your answers to questions 1 and 2 in Exercise 5. Guess the meaning of the expressions in *italics*.

❝I've been with the Austin Police Department for thirteen-and-a-half years. *Currently* I'm assigned to *crimes against property*, the theft division. Theft entails several areas: we investigate *white collar crime*, we investigate property crimes, we investigate anything to do with *embezzlements* or any kind of stolen property – we *investigate* all those types of crimes.❞

7 📼 Now listen to Part 2 of the interview. Cathy is telling a story about something that happened while she was on patrol. After you listen, complete this summary with the correct form of the verbs.

While she [1]..... (work) on patrol a few years ago, Cathy [2]..... (receive) a call from a woman who [3]..... (be) very upset. She said that someone [4]..... (hide) in her home, so Cathy [5]..... (drive) to her apartment. While they [6]..... (talk), the woman suddenly [7]..... (shout), 'They're in there, they're in there'. The two women [8]..... (creep) through the apartment and as they [9]..... (walk) across it in the dark, the wind [10]..... (blow) a curtain into Cathy's face. Cathy [11]..... (pull) out her gun and almost [12]..... (shoot) the curtain, but there [13]..... (be) nobody there.

A short talk

GETTING STARTED

1 Who are the people in this picture?

1 Where did they live?
2 What do you know about them? Where does your information come from?
3 Which are usually the heroes? Do you agree that they were heroes? Why/why not?
4 Think of famous people in your country's history. Were they heroes or criminals?

READING

2 Read the text above about a man who is famous in Britain. Say why he is famous and then answer the questions.

1 When and where did Robin Hood live?
2 What kind of 'crimes' did he commit?
3 Who benefited from these 'crimes'?

3 Look back at the text and answer these questions.

1 Which words and phrases tell us that Robin Hood possibly did not exist?
2 Which of the words below usually have:
   a) a positive meaning?
   b) a negative meaning?
   c) either a positive or a negative meaning, depending on the speaker?
   hero   rebel   criminal   authority
   outlaw   justice
3 What is a 'people's hero'?

ROBIN HOOD: fact or fiction?

Robin Hood was apparently a fourteenth-century English hero. People of that time sang songs about his adventures, although the most famous stories come from the sixteenth century and later. In the twentieth century a television series and several films have helped to continue the legend.

Robin Hood was a rebel and in many ways a criminal, but he was a people's hero. The legend says that he lived in the forest with his companions, his 'merry men'. They robbed and killed representatives of authority in order to give the money to the poor. His main enemy was the Sheriff of Nottingham, a

4 How would these people describe Robin Hood? Use words from Exercise 3 and any others you know.

1 one of his companions
2 a poor person to whom he gave money
3 the Sheriff of Nottingham

DEVELOPING VOCABULARY

5 Explain the meanings of these expressions.

1 landowners
   Landowners are people who …
2 the poor

What expressions can we use to describe:

3 people who own their own homes?
   home owners
4 people who own factories?
5 people who own cars?
6 rich people?
7 famous people?
8 young people?

local government representative, but he also stole from rich landowners and members of the church. According to the legend, he was always kind and polite to women (including his female companion, Maid Marian) and to the poor.

Historical 'detectives' have tried to find evidence for a real Robin Hood with little success. There *was* an outlaw of that name, who lived outside the law because of his crimes, but we do not know much about him. What is certain is that for people of that period and later times, Robin Hood was a symbol of justice; of their impatience with authoritarian government and unfair laws. New stories about him have appeared through the centuries, and he has become a legendary figure.

LISTENING

6 📼 **Listen to a story about Robin Hood. Then work in pairs and put these events in the order they actually happened.**

a) Robin gives the knight money.
b) Robin lends the knight money.
c) The knight's son kills someone.
d) Robin and his men rob some rich travellers.
e) Robin and his men invite the knight to eat with them.
f) The knight brings money to Robin.
g) The knight gives money to the rich landowner.

7 📼 **Listen again.**

1 Make notes on the details; write down all the important words and phrases.

2 Compare your notes with your partner's and add any information that you have not got.

3 Listen again. Which of these linking words and phrases refer to:
a) time?   b) cause and effect?
one day ...   so ...   when ...   as a result ...   the next day ...
until ...   in the meantime ...   a few weeks later ...   because ...

SPEAKING

8 **Take it in turns to tell the story in the past tense. Use your notes and the linking phrases from Exercise 7 to help you. Start like this:**
I'll tell you a story about Robin Hood. One day ...

9 **Work in groups. List some legendary figures in your own or other cultures. Then make notes about each one in answer to these questions.**

1 Where was he/she from?
2 When was he/she alive?
3 Why is he/she famous?
4 Did he/she really exist?
5 What kind of person was he/she?
6 What kind of things did he/she do?
7 Did he/she act alone or with other people?
8 Has he/she become a symbol? If so, of what?

10 **Remind each other of stories about these people. Help each other to add as much detail as possible.**

11 **Now work in pairs. Choose one of the figures and prepare to tell the class about that person. Practise your talk in two parts:**

1 a general introduction to the person's life and reputation
2 a story about one particular event

12 **Talk to the class. Remember to speak slowly and clearly, and use your voice to make the story dramatic.**
Student A: Give the general introduction to the person's life.
Student B: Tell the story.

Language reference

GRAMMAR

1 The past simple

USES

- We use the past simple to talk about a complete action or event, or a state, at a specific time in the past.
  EXAMPLES: *We **bought** a new car. She **worked** for a TV company.*
- We also use it to talk about a series of events.
  EXAMPLE: *I **found** a jug and **filled** it with water.*
- The past simple is often used with a past time adverbial.
  EXAMPLE: *My parents arrived in Britain **yesterday.***

FORMS

- Regular verbs in the past simple affirmative:
  infinitive + *ed*   *work – work**ed***
  infinitive ending in *e* + *d*   *like – lik**ed***
  infinitive ending in *y* = ⱄ + *ied*   *hurry – hurr**ied***
  many verbs ending in one consonant = the same consonant again + *ed*
  *stop – stop**ped***
- Here are the forms of common irregular verbs:

	past		past		past		past
be	was/were	eat	ate	make	made	sleep	slept
become	became	find	found	meet	met	speak	spoke
begin	began	get	got	pay	paid	spend	spent
bring	brought	give	gave	put	put	stand	stood
build	built	go	went	read	read	take	took
buy	bought	have	had	say	said	teach	taught
come	came	keep	kept	see	saw	tell	told
do	did	know	knew	sell	sold	think	thought
drink	drank	learn	learnt	send	sent	wear	wore
drive	drove	leave	left	shut	shut	write	wrote

- We use *did (not)* + infinitive (without *to*) for questions and negative forms.
  EXAMPLES: ***Did** you **have** fun? I **didn't meet** anyone.*
  Modals and *was/were* form questions and negatives without an auxiliary.
  EXAMPLES: ***Was** Sue there? She **couldn't** come.*

2 The past progressive

USES

We use the past progressive:

- to emphasise that a past situation was continuous or temporary.
  EXAMPLE: *I **was working** there in 1989.*
- to describe a situation that was in progress at a particular time. We often use *while* before a past progressive clause or *when* before a past simple clause.
  EXAMPLES: *We **were walking** along the street **when** we heard a loud noise. They **were playing** squash at six o'clock.*
- to describe two or more situations that were in progress at the same time. We often use *while* to join the clauses.
  EXAMPLE: *Jenny **was working while** I **was watching** TV.*

FORMS

- The past progressive is formed from the past tense of the verb *to be* + an *–ing* verb form.
  EXAMPLE: *My friends **were waiting** for me.*
- Questions and negative statements are formed in the same way as in the present progressive.
  EXAMPLES: ***Were** you **waiting** for me? I **wasn't waiting**.*

3 Reflexive pronouns

USES

Reflexive pronouns are used:

- With certain verbs, when the object of the verb is the same as the subject.
  EXAMPLES: *I'm drying **myself**. Can you introduce **yourselves**?*
- To emphasise the subject of a sentence.
  EXAMPLE: *They did it **themselves**.*

FORMS

- Singular reflexive pronouns end in *–self: myself, yourself, himself, herself, itself*.
- Plural forms end in *–selves: ourselves, yourselves, themselves*.
- *I, you* and *we* form reflexive pronouns with possessive adjectives: *my + self, your/our + selves. He, she, it* and *they* form them with object pronouns: *him/her/it + self, them + selves.*

FUNCTIONAL LANGUAGE

1 Agreeing with someone
I agree with you.
We all share your opinion.
I think you're absolutely right.

2 Disagreeing with someone
I don't agree with you.
I disagree with Mike.
It's wrong to say that women need protection.

Talkback

What's your story?

🔊 **Look at these pictures and listen to the cassette.**

1 Which picture is the speaker referring to?
2 Work with a partner. Choose one of the pictures and compose a story that is believable (like the example). Make notes and be prepared to tell your story to the class.
3 Tell your story to the class. Compare it with the stories of others who have chosen the same situation.

The science of shopping

GETTING STARTED

1 When we go shopping for food, we like to believe that we buy only what we *want* to buy. But do we? Think about a large supermarket near you, and discuss these questions with a partner.

1 Where is the entrance to the shop? Is there a reason, do you think?
2 What does the supermarket display near the entrance? Why?
3 Where are basic foods like sugar and tea? Are they near each other?
4 Do you move more quickly or more slowly if there is a lot of space between shelves?
5 Where do staff put large quantities of a product that they want to sell quickly?
6 Are the shelves full at all times?

READING

2 Read an extract from a newspaper article about supermarkets. How well does it describe your local supermarket? Are there other factors that you think are important?

The story behind supermarket success

ARE supermarkets designed to persuade us to buy more? When you enter a supermarket, the manager knows better than you do how you will behave – which way you will walk, where you will look, what will make you buy one product rather than another. When customers go into a shop, they naturally look to their left but move clockwise, towards the right. So supermarket entrances are usually on the left of the building, and the layout is designed to take shoppers around the store, aisle after aisle, from left to right. Then shoppers will pay attention to all the products.

Fresh fruit and vegetables are displayed near supermarket entrances. This gives the impression that only healthy food is sold in the shop. Basic foods that everyone buys, like sugar and tea, are not put near each other. They are kept in different aisles so customers are taken past other attractive foods before they find what they want. In this way, shoppers are encouraged to buy products that they do not really need.

People walk quickly through narrow aisles, but they move more slowly in wide aisles and give more attention to the products. One best-selling position for products is at the end of aisles, because shoppers slow down to turn into the next aisle. Another is on shelves at eye level. Supermarkets are paid by food manufacturers to put their products in each of these high-selling places.

Sweets are often placed at children's eye level at the checkout. While parents are waiting to pay, children reach for the sweets and put them in the trolley.

More is bought from a fifteen-foot display of one type of product (e.g. cereals, washing powder) than from a ten-foot one. Customers also buy more when shelves are full than when they are half empty. They do not like to buy from shelves with few products on them because they feel there is something wrong with those products that are there.

3 Match the following features of a supermarket with the labels on the picture.

1 the entrance	4 shoppers	7 trolleys
2 a narrow aisle	5 shelves	8 a special display
3 a wide aisle	6 the checkout	

DISCOVERING LANGUAGE

4 Look at these examples of passive verb forms from the article.

A *Fresh fruit and vegetables **are displayed** near supermarket entrances.*

B *Basic foods ... **are not put** near each other.*

C ***Are** supermarkets **designed** to persuade us ... ?*

1 Find other examples in the article.

2 Complete this rule about the form of the present simple passive:
It is formed with the present tense of the verb *to* ..... + a ..... .

3 Look at two sentences with a similar meaning. Why do you think the journalist has used a passive verb form in a)?
   a) Sweets are often placed at children's eye-level.
   b) Supermarket staff often place sweets at children's eye-level.

WRITING

5 The diagram below explains how green beans from Kenya in Africa arrive on the shelves of a British supermarket. Continue this description of the process:

The beans are grown in Kenya. On Day 1 they are picked in the morning and taken to ...

take	
PACKING HOUSE *weigh pack*	Day 1
put	
COLD STORAGE	
drive	
NAIROBI AIRPORT	
fly	Day 2
LONDON	
CUSTOMS *inspect*	
transport	Day 3
CENTRAL SUPERMARKET STORE	
distribute	Day 4
Supermarket Supermarket	

SPEAKING

6 Work with your partner. Make a list of the main foods you eat. Are they imported or are they grown/made in your country? How are they processed?

Focus

TOPICS
• Cars
• Production of cars
• Advertising

GRAMMAR
• *Both, neither,*
  (...nor), all, none

SKILLS
• Listening:
  interview extracts
• Speaking: role play

SPEECH PATTERNS
• Sentence stress
  with *both ... and,*
  neither ... nor, all,
  none

Making a sale

🖾 Documentary

LISTENING

1 Before you listen, look at the pictures from the brochure of a car manufacturer.

1 What kind of car is advertised?

2 What kind of image do you think the company wants to create? Choose adjectives from this list to help you:

international   British   handmade   practical
modern   cheap   safe   expensive   mass produced
luxurious   traditional   sensible   fun   attractive
comfortable   reliable   environmentally-friendly (green)

2 🖾 Charles Morgan (below) is the Production Manager of the Morgan Motor Company. Listen to the first part of an interview with him and answer the questions.

1 What relation is Charles to the person who started the company?

2 How many people are employed in the factory?

3 The cars are 'coach-built'.
   What does this mean?

3 🖾 Listen to the second part of the interview.

1 There is a ticket on each car in the factory. What is written on it?

2 Which of these parts does Charles Morgan say are made by the company?
   a) the engine
   b) the fuel tank
   c) the brakes
   d) the radiator

3 What percentage of Morgan cars are exported?

4 According to Charles Morgan, in what ways is a Morgan car unique?

4 Compare the Morgan with other types of car that you know well.

1 Why do you think people choose a Morgan car? Would you like one? Why?

2 Do you prefer things that are handmade or things that are mass produced? Have you got anything that is handmade?

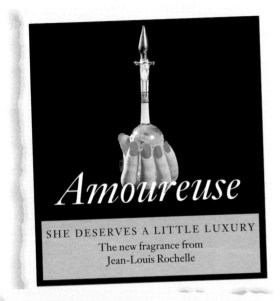

Amoureuse

SHE DESERVES A LITTLE LUXURY
The new fragrance from
Jean-Louis Rochelle

A NECKLACE OF DISTINCTION

Hand-crafted solid
silver jewellery
by Parrajo of Mexico

5 Look at these advertisements and at the brochure for Morgan cars. What do you think these products have in common?

DISCOVERING LANGUAGE

6 Read these statements about the three products.

A **Both** the car **and** the necklace are handmade.
B **Both** of them are handmade.
C **Neither** the necklace **nor** the perfume is British.
D **Neither** of them is British.
E **All** of them are expensive.
F **None** of them is cheap.

1 Which of the words in bold refer to *two* objects? Which words refer to more than two?
2 Which words are followed by a singular verb?

SPEECH PATTERNS

7 📼 Listen to the sentences in Exercise 6 and underline the words that are stressed. Say which two sentences have a different stress pattern from the others. Then listen again and repeat.

8 Work in groups. Write down the names of three products (e.g. food) that are widely advertised in your country. Use the structures in Exercise 6 to compare:

a) the products   b) the advertisements

SPEAKING

9 Work in groups. You work for an advertising company and your job is to sell a computer to as many different groups of people as possible.

1 Which types of software (a–g) do you think would appeal to:
  1 teenagers?
  2 parents buying for children?
  3 business people?
  a) word-processing
  b) games
  c) design
  d) accounts and book-keeping
  e) home study
  f) music-making
  g) desktop publishing

Write your answers in the first column of a chart like the one below.

2 Which qualities of the computer do you think attract these three groups? Add adjectives from the list in Exercise 1 and any others you can think of to the second column of your chart.

	SOFTWARE	QUALITIES OF THE COMPUTER
teenagers		
parents buying for children		
people in business		

10 Work in pairs.

Student A: You are a salesperson. Try to sell the computer to Student B. Use your imagination to describe its features.

Student B: Choose one of the three roles in the chart. Ask about the features of the computer that interest you.

Letters

Focus

TOPIC
- Sales

FUNCTIONS
- Letter-writing conventions

SKILLS
- Reading: letters, a memo, an invoice, an order form
- Writing: formal letters, form completion
- Speaking: discussion

GETTING STARTED

1 Look at the picture and consider these questions.

1 What business is the woman in?
2 How does she sell her products?
3 What is special about them?
4 Are there words or pictures on any of your clothes?
5 Why do people like wearing clothes with words on?
6 What would your reaction be if you saw people wearing the T-shirts in the picture?

READING

2 People who run small businesses regularly receive different kinds of letter. Before you read, list the kinds of letter that you think Sandra, the woman in the picture, might get, and who she might get them from.

FROM: customer
KIND OF LETTER: order for a T-shirt

A

Order form

Description	Brochure number	Number of items	Price	Lettering
Black, small, short-sleeved	2065B	1	£15.99	I'm older than I look!

B

Sandra,   10.15 a.m.

Accountant rang to say he needs to speak to you urgently. Can you phone him some time today?

3 Look at the correspondence Sandra received one morning.

1 Which papers were in the same envelope?
2 Do you think she knows the person who wrote them? How do you know?
3 Who are they from? What is the purpose of each?
4 Which letters do you think Sandra was expecting?

C

INVOICE

002640		14th November

To: Ms S Taylor	From:	RG Wholesalers
T-shirts by Mail		49 Bleak Street
Unit E, Railway Estate		Frinton-on-Sea
Nottingham		Essex

For: Supply of T-shirts

100 (medium white) at £6.50		£650.00
100 (medium blue) at £6.70		£670.00
150 (small white) at £6.00		£900.00
100 (large black) at £6.90		£690.00
Total		**£2910.00**

D

```
                    4 The Court
                    Leafield LF2 1BC
                    15th November 199-

Dear Ms Taylor

I'm writing to complain about
a T-shirt I bought recently
from your company.

    Although I am happy with the
quality of the shirt itself, I
cannot say the same about the
lettering.

    I have just washed it and
some of the letters have
peeled off. I find this
unacceptable.

    I enclose the T-shirt.
Please send a full refund of
£18.99 by return of post.

Yours sincerely

Erica Patterson
```

44

4 Imagine you are Sandra. In which order will you deal with the correspondence? Why?

FOCUS ON FUNCTIONS

5 Consider these questions about letter-writing conventions.

1 Where does the date appear in relation to the sender's address?
2 Add a number (1,2,3,4) to each abbreviation to form a date.
   a) th   b) nd   c) st   d) rd
3 Now abbreviate these dates:
   a) January the ninth
   b) October the twenty-second
   c) April the first
   d) February the twenty-third
4 Match the openings with an ending.
   Dear (name)   Yours faithfully
   Dear Sir/Madam   Yours sincerely
5 Find three ways of making polite requests.

READING

6 Look at Letter E. Identify the parts of the letter in which the writer:

a) gives his reason for writing.
b) closes the letter.
c) gives the message to be included.
d) writes his own address and the date.
e) gives the address and date for delivery.
f) says that the order form and payment are enclosed.
g) opens the letter.
h) writes the address of the person he is writing to.

SPEAKING

7 Work with your partner. You decide to send a T-shirt with a message on the front (and back?) to a mutual friend.

1 Decide on a reason for sending this. (Is it a birthday present? A wedding gift? A leaving present?)
2 Think of all the messages you have seen on T-shirts and make up an original one together. Try to make it amusing.

WRITING

8 Now order the T-shirt for your friend.

1 Copy and complete an order form like A.
2 Write a message to your friend for *T-shirts by Mail* to include in the package.
3 Write a letter to accompany your order form. Use Letter E as a guide.

9 Write Sandra's reply to Letter D. Apologise for the problems and repay the money.

Here are some useful ways of apologising:
I am terribly sorry that ...
I apologise for (+ noun/-ing) ...
Please accept my apologies.
I hope you will accept my apologies.

E

6 Elgin Place **(1)**
Southport
November 15th

T-Shirts by Mail **(2)**
Unit E, Railway Estate
Nottingham

Dear Sir/Madam **(3)**

I'm writing to order a T-shirt from your brochure. **(4)**

I enclose the order form and a cheque for £15.99. **(5)**

As the T-shirt is a birthday gift for a friend, could **(6)** you please include the following message:

Have a wonderful day. I'm sorry I can't be with you. See you soon. Love David.

Please send it to the following address to arrive **(7)** before December 6th:

Jane Bradley, 116 Lower Street, London, NW6 3EJ.

Yours faithfully **(8)**

David Jenson

F

R G Wholesalers
IMPORTED TEXTILES
49 Bleak Street, Frinton-on-Sea, Essex

14th November

Dear Sandra,

Here's the invoice you asked for.
I'm sorry it's so late.

See you soon.

Jeff

Language reference

1 The present simple passive

USES

We use present passive forms:

- when we do not know who performs an action.
  EXAMPLE: *Bags **are** often **stolen** from cafés and shops.*
- when this information is uninteresting, unimportant or obvious.
  EXAMPLE: *These apples **are grown** in Britain.*

In English, the most important information is often at the beginning of a sentence. Compare the emphasis in these sentences:

Active   *A lot of people in Britain **eat** pasta.*
Passive   *Pasta **is eaten** by a lot of people in Britain.*

Passive forms are often used to describe processes.
EXAMPLE: *The jeans **are sent** from the factory to the warehouse. They **are** then **delivered** …*

FORMS

- The present simple passive is formed with the present tense of the verb *to be* + a past participle.
  EXAMPLE: *Fish **is imported** from France.*
- We use *by* if we want to say who performs the action.
  EXAMPLES: *The fruit is picked **by** students. The cars are built **by** skilled craftsmen.*

2 *Both, neither, none, all*

USES

- *Both* and *neither* refer to two people or things. When they are used with countable nouns, *all* and *none* refer to a number of people or things.
- These words are often used for emphasis.
  EXAMPLE: *'I don't think many people are coming.' 'You're probably right. **None** of my friends is coming.'*

FORMS

- All these words can be followed by *of* + object.
  EXAMPLE: ***Both of them** are coming.*
- *Both* and *all* take a plural verb because they refer to more than one person or thing.
  EXAMPLE: *All of them **live** here.*
- *Neither* takes a singular verb because the meaning is *not one*.
  EXAMPLE: *Neither of them **is** the right colour.*
  It is often used with *nor*, which means *and not*.
  EXAMPLE: ***Neither** the blue one **nor** the green one matches the walls.*

- *None* can take a singular or plural verb, although some people think that the use of a singular verb is more correct.
  EXAMPLE: *None of them **is/are** exactly what I want.*
- We can also use *both, neither* and *all* before a noun phrase without *of*.
  EXAMPLES: *I'll ring **both the cinemas. Neither class** has room for me. **All the trains** are late today.*
- We can use *both* and *all* on their own for emphasis when it is clear who or what they refer to.
  EXAMPLE: *There's no answer. I suppose they're **all** out.*
- *All* and *none* can also be used with uncountable nouns.
  EXAMPLE: *We drank **all the orange juice.***
  In this case, they both take a singular verb.
  EXAMPLE: ***None** of the milk **is** drinkable.*

FUNCTIONAL LANGUAGE

1 Opening and closing formal letters
Dear Sir/Madam – Yours faithfully
Dear Mr Jensen – Yours sincerely

2 Apologising in formal letters
I'm (terribly) sorry that you were disappointed.
I apologise for the poor quality of your T-shirt.
Please accept my apologies.
I hope you will accept my apologies.

Progress check Units 4–5

GRAMMAR AND FUNCTIONS

1 Complete these questions and answers about a man called William Tell.

Who was William Tell?
He was a legendary Swiss hero.

1 *When* ..... *?* In the 13th and early 14th centuries.
2 *What* ..... *?* He was a peasant and a huntsman.
3 Did he like the Austrian rulers of his country? *No,* ..... .
4 What did the Austrians try to do? *They* ..... *to capture him.*
5 Why is he still so famous? *Because Schiller* ..... *a play about him.*
6 Didn't Rossini write an opera about him too? *Yes,* ..... .

2 Complete the story with past simple or past progressive verb forms.

One day, William Tell and his young son Walter [1]..... (walk) through the village of Altdorf when two Austrian soldiers [2]..... (arrest) him. Gessler, the Austrian governor, [3]..... (ride) through the village at that moment. He [4]..... (order) Tell to shoot an apple from his son's head. While little Walter [5]..... (prepare) himself, his father [6]..... (take out) two arrows. He [7]..... (shoot) one into the centre of the apple. Everyone [8]..... (still/ applaud) Tell's skill when Gessler [9]..... (ask) about the second arrow. 'You are lucky that my son is alive, ' Tell [10]..... (say). 'This one [11]..... (be) for you.'

3 Complete the text with an active or passive form of the verb in brackets.

Basic foods differ throughout the world. Rice and noodles [1]..... (eat) in south-east Asia, while bread [2]..... (be) more common in Arab countries. Europeans also [3]..... (eat) a lot of bread, but potatoes [4]..... (grow) everywhere. In Italy, pasta [5]..... (use) as the main ingredient of many dishes. In some north African countries, couscous is very popular. Couscous [6]..... (make) from semolina.

4 Complete these dialogues with reflexive pronouns (*myself*, etc.).

1 A: Have you hurt ..... ?
  B: I've cut ..... , but it isn't serious.
2 A: Did you all enjoy ..... ?
  B: We always enjoy ..... on holiday!
3 A: Should children learn how to protect ..... ?
  B: I think so. My daughter can already defend ..... , and my son is teaching ..... karate.

5 Look at the picture. Correct the sentences.

All of these people are female.
One of these people is female.

1 None of these people is young.
2 Neither of the men is wearing a jacket.
3 Both of them have long hair.
4 None of them is drinking.
5 One man is not carrying a bag; all the other people are.
6 All of them are smoking.

VOCABULARY

6 Complete these crime reports.

1 Last night two men broke into Lansdowne Primary School and ..... six computers. A neighbour saw them putting the equipment into a van and reported the ..... , but the men escaped before the police arrived.
2 A family escaped with minor injuries after someone ..... fire to their house. They believe that the ..... is a local teenager.
3 Gang members ..... two shops in the High Street in the early hours of the morning. Police think they are the same people who ..... an old man just after midnight and left him lying in the street.

6 Body and mind

Staying well

Focus

TOPIC
- Health and fitness

GRAMMAR
- First conditional
- Second conditional

SKILLS
- Reading: a magazine article
- Speaking: role play

VOCABULARY DEVELOPMENT
- Prefix *over-*
- Suffix *-able*

GETTING STARTED

1 We all get ill from time to time, but most of us try to stay in good health. Magazines and newspapers often give advice on health. Look at the headlines.

> **Are you getting enough sleep?**

> **You are what you eat**

> **YOUR SKIN HATES JUNK FOOD!**

> *Do you really want to smell like an ashtray?*

> Jog your way to a healthy heart

> **Meditation – the answer to life's pressures**

Work with a partner and list all the advice you can think of for staying healthy.

You should eat lots of fruit and vegetables.

2 Tell your partner what *you* do to stay healthy.

I do weightlifting twice a week. I don't smoke.

READING

3 Before you read, look at the title and picture in the article on the right.

1 What are these people doing?
2 What information do you think is in the article?
3 List five words or phrases that you think are in the article.
4 Read the article and see if you were right.

4 Which of these opinions are expressed in the article? Which ones do *you* agree with?

1 Adults do not get enough exercise.
2 Small children do not get enough exercise.
3 Babies need to do exercises.
4 Children should have a better diet.
5 People need training in parenting skills.

5 List all the words and phrases that refer to young children.

DEVELOPING VOCABULARY

6 Guess the meaning of these words from the article, and check with a dictionary. What are the meanings of *-able* and *over-* ?

disposable   washable
overweight

Now guess the meanings of the words in *italics*.

1 an *enjoyable* evening
2 a *profitable* business
3 *dependable* staff
4 *overworked* teachers
5 *overpopulated* areas
6 an *overloaded* bus

Fit for life

Fashions in child-care, as all parents know, come and go. Bottle-feeding or mother's milk? Disposable nappies or washable towels? Full-time parental care or a child-minder? And now, following the publication of a new book called Childsplay, *do the under-fives need exercise routines?*

DISCOVERING LANGUAGE

7 Look at this conditional sentence from the article:

… if small children take no regular exercise, bad habits will continue into adulthood.

1 Which verb structures are used in the two clauses?
2 Which clause expresses:
   a) a condition?   b) a consequence?
3 Complete this sentence, using the first conditional:
   If toddlers ..... (do) exercises, they ..... (stay) fit.
4 Does the first conditional express a condition that is likely or unlikely?

8 Now look at these sentences from the article:

If the world were a safer place, every child would run around freely, …

They would not be overweight if they ate healthier food.

1 Which verb structures are used in each clause?
2 Which clause expresses:
   a) a condition?   b) a consequence?
3 What do you notice about the past form of *to be* in the *if* clause?
4 Complete this sentence, using the second conditional:
   If there ..... (be) no cars, children ..... (play) in the street.
5 Does the second conditional express conditions that are likely, unlikely or unreal?

9 Now use your imagination to finish these second conditional sentences.

1 If I had a small child, …
2 If children didn't watch television, …
3 If they played in the streets, …
4 If parents didn't listen to experts, …
5 Children would be fit and healthy …
6 They wouldn't have a bad diet …
7 Teenagers would be healthier …
8 If I found my child with a cigarette, …

SPEAKING

10 People often worry about relatives who smoke. What arguments could you use to persuade a relative to stop smoking?

If you stopped smoking, you'd be much healthier.
You'll damage your lungs if you don't stop smoking!

Think of excuses that your relative might make to justify smoking.

I'd be irritable if I stopped smoking.

Role play the situation.
Student A: You are a smoker. Think of some clever excuses!
Student B: You are a non-smoking relative. Be persuasive.

The author of *Childsplay*, Lucy Jackson, believes that they do. Most schoolchildren do some sport at school, and many adults take regular exercise in their free time. Toddlers, though, spend most of the time in front of the television or sitting in a pushchair and/or high chair. If the world were a safer place, every child would run around freely, but that is simply not possible. As a result, they become inactive, overweight and unfit.

Ms Jackson is worried that if small children take no regular exercise, bad habits will continue into adulthood. She suggests that parents should begin exercises with very small babies, moving their legs and arms gently in time to music. As children grow, they should follow an exercise programme using soft balls, household furniture and play equipment.

Many experts in child development are not convinced. They feel that children will learn to run and jump as they play naturally; they do not need structured exercise. They would not be overweight if they ate healthier food. An increasing number of parents, though, are taking their youngsters to exercise classes. The tots jump around with their mothers to disco music. They seem to enjoy themselves, but it is not at all clear if the classes have any effect on their future development. ■

Treatment

GETTING STARTED

1 **Look at these words:**

optician   pharmacist   surgeon   acupuncturist
dentist   psychiatrist   herbalist

Who would you see if you:

a) had toothache?
   If I had toothache, I'd see a dentist.
b) needed an operation?
c) were extremely unhappy?
d) had bad eyesight?
e) wanted natural medicines from plants?
f) wanted treatment with needles?
g) needed medicine for a minor problem?

2 **Match these words for health problems with the pictures.**

an ache   a pain   a cut   a sting

 A   B  C  D

How would each person describe their problem? Choose one or more phrases from each of Lists A and B.

LIST A
I've cut myself.   I've got a headache.   I've broken my arm.
A bee's stung me.   I've got a pain in my …

LIST B
It aches.   It's sore.   It's bleeding.   It hurts.   It's painful.

⟳ COMPARING CULTURES

3 **Look at this picture of a doctor's waiting room.**

1 What point is the artist making about doctors' surgeries in Britain.
2 Is this true in your country? How long must you wait on average? Is it necessary to make an appointment?

LISTENING

4 **A patient is consulting his doctor.**

1 Work in pairs. Listen to Part 1 of the conversation. Then list the questions that you think the doctor will ask.
2 Listen to Part 2 of the conversation and compare your questions with the doctor's.
3 Decide what advice the doctor will give. Listen to Part 3 and check.
4 Do you ever feel like this? What do you do when you feel tired?

FOCUS ON FUNCTIONS

5 **Look at these extracts from the conversation:**

*People of your age **ought to** sleep for at least seven hours a night.*
*You **should** start to take some exercise.*
*You certainly **ought not to** drink coffee before going to bed.*
*You **shouldn't** worry so much.*

1 What is the function of the words in **bold**?
2 What form of the verb follows:
   a) should?   b) ought?
3 How is the negative of each verb formed?

SPEAKING

6 Work in pairs.

Student A: You are a patient. You have a pain somewhere. Think about the details of your problem.

Student B: You are the doctor. Your patient is in pain. Think about the questions you want to ask and what you want to say. Use these guidelines to help you:

BASIC INFORMATION	REASSURANCE
What ... ?	*Don't worry. It's ...*
Where exactly ... ?	

MORE DETAILS	ADVICE
How long ... ?	*You should ...*
How bad ... ?	*You ought to ...*

▣ Documentary

LISTENING

7 Before you listen, look at the picture.

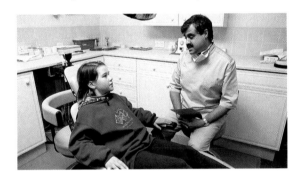

1 What is this man's job?
2 What is he doing at the moment?
3 Find these words in your dictionary. Put them in order of the strength of fear from least to greatest. (least) *uneasy*
   frightened   terrified   nervous   petrified
   uneasy   worried   anxious
4 How do you think the girl in the picture feels? How do *you* feel at the dentist's?

8 Mubarak Samji is a British dentist. Listen and answer the questions.

1 Why are people frightened of dental treatment?
2 Which of these methods does Mr Samji say he uses to calm people?
   a) soft music   d) no treatment
   b) a local anaesthetic   e) tranquillisers
   c) a general anaesthetic
3 What advice does he give children?
   You should ...   You shouldn't ...

FOCUS ON FUNCTIONS

9 ▤ Listen to a conversation with another dentist. Which expressions do you hear?

Don't worry.   I'm afraid of ...   Don't cry.
Don't be afraid.   Calm down.   It'll be all right.
Relax.   I'm worried about ...   I'm frightened of ...

Now group all the expressions into ways of:

a) describing fear
b) calming and reassuring someone

DEVELOPING VOCABULARY

10 Look again at the ways of expressing fear in Exercise 9.

1 Notice this construction: fear adjective + preposition + *-ing* form.
2 Check your dictionary and find the prepositions that follow the adjectives in Exercise 7.
3 Write sentences about your fears, using these phrases.
   I'm nervous about travelling on underground trains.

SPEECH PATTERNS

11 ▤ Listen. Does the speaker's voice move up or down at the end of these expressions? Match each intonation pattern with a group of expressions.

A ⌐

Don't worry.
It'll be all right.
Don't be afraid.
Don't cry.

B ⌐

Calm down.
Relax.

Practise saying each expression, then listen again and repeat.

SPEAKING

12 Work with a partner.

Student A: You are worried about something that you have to do (e.g. flying, giving a talk, taking an exam). Tell your partner about your fears.

Student B: Try to calm your friend and persuade him/her that there's nothing to be afraid of. Give some advice.

Start like this:

A: *I'm terribly worried!*
B: *Why? What's the matter?*

Then change roles.

Creating a mood

Focus

TOPICS
- Sounds
- Ghost stories
- Fear

SKILLS
- Listening: sounds, a sound sequence
- Reading: a literary extract
- Writing: a story

✪ COMPARING CULTURES

1 📼 In every language there are words that sound like particular noises. In English, for example, the sound of the word *Bang!* is like the sound of a gunshot.

1 The words below describe sounds. Say them aloud. Then listen to the cassette and match them to the sounds.

a) scream   g) rustle
b) creak   h) smash
c) whisper   i) rumble
d) crack   j) drip
e) bump   k) splash
f) growl   l) cough

2 Check the meanings of these words in a dictionary. How similar are they to words in your language that describe the same noises?

READING: A LITERARY EXTRACT

2 Before you read, think of a ghost story – a film, play or book – that contains a scene in which someone is terrified. List words and phrases to describe:

a) the setting: *a dark night, an empty house*
b) the atmosphere: *silent, frightening*
c) how people or animals reacted to fear: *they ran, their hair stood on end*

Compare notes with a partner and add other words and phrases to your list.

3 Read an extract from a ghost story called *The Woman in Black*. Can you find any of the expressions on your list?

---

108   *The Woman in Black*

At first, all seemed very quiet, very still, and I wondered why I had awoken. Then, with a missed heartbeat, I realised that Spider was up and standing at the door. Every hair of her body was on end, her ears were pricked, her tail erect, the whole of her tense, as if ready to spring. And she was emitting a soft, low growl from deep in her throat. I sat up, paralysed, frozen, in the bed, conscious only of the dog and of the prickling of my own skin and of what suddenly seemed a different kind of silence, ominous and dreadful. And then, from somewhere within the depths of the house – but somewhere not very far from the room in which I was – I heard a noise. It was a faint noise, and, although I strained my ears, I could not make out exactly what it was. It was a sound like a regular yet intermittent bump or rumble. Nothing else happened. There were no footsteps, no creaking floorboards, the air was absolutely still, the wind did not moan through the casement. Only the muffled noise went on and the dog continued to stand, bristling at the door, now putting her nose to the gap at the bottom and snuffling along, now taking a pace backwards, head cocked and, like me, listening, listening. And, every so often, she growled again.

The author of *The Woman in Black*, Susan Hill, is an English novelist and children's writer. She is also a radio broadcaster and a regular reviewer of fiction for national newspapers. A stage version of *The Woman in Black* has become extremely popular throughout Britain.

4 Now answer these questions about the story.

1 Who was Spider?
2 Why did the man wake up?
3 Where were they?
4 Why were they frightened?
5 What did they both do next?
6 What do we know about the weather?

5 Find the words in *italics* below in the story and answer the questions.

1 These words all have more or less the same meaning. What is it?
on end   pricked   erect
2 What is the effect on your body if you are:
paralysed with fear?
frozen with fear?
tense?
3 What kind of noises do you think these are?
a *faint* noise
a *muffled* noise
the *moaning* of the wind
the *snuffling* of a dog at the door

6 Look back at the sequence of events in the story.

1 Which words and phrases does the writer use to make the sequence clear?
2 What other words and phrases can you use?
3 Use your list to describe these events in the order they happened:
a) He heard the sound for the first time.
b) The dog went to the door.
c) He sat up in bed.
d) The man woke up.
e) He couldn't hear anything.

7 Look at this sentence from the story. What does *like* mean here?

*It was a sound **like** a regular yet intermittent bump or rumble.*

Like is often used to compare one thing with another:

*It was a sound **like** a tap dripping.*

*He had skin **like** marble, smooth and white with a faint shine.*

Use your imagination to complete these sentences with a comparison.

1 The house was like …
2 His eyes were like …
3 It was a sound like …
4 She had a voice like …

8 Work in pairs. Use your imagination to add to the story.

1 How do you picture the scene described in the story?
a) How big is the house?
b) How is the room furnished?
c) What is the dog like?
d) How old is the man?
2 What do you think is the cause of the noise?
3 What do you think is going to happen next?

LISTENING

9 ▭ Listen to how the story continues.

1 Write words from Exercise 1 that describe the noises you hear.
2 Listen again and make notes about what happened in each part.
1 man got out of bed, floorboards creaked, man coughed, …
3 Now listen to the whole sequence again and think about the man's feelings.

WRITING

10 Work with a partner. Imagine you are the person in the story. Continue the story from the end of the extract opposite. Use your notes from Exercise 9 and appropriate sequencing words.

• Write the story from the man's point of view, using the pronoun *I*.
• Recreate the tension in the story by telling the reader about your feelings, the sounds you heard, the way the dog behaved.
• Give the story an ending.
I got out of bed slowly and quietly. When I put my feet on the floor, the floorboards creaked …

Language reference

1 First conditional sentences

USES

- We use the first conditional to talk about the consequences of a possible future event or situation.
  EXAMPLE: *If the weather's fine, we'll have a picnic.*
- Functional uses of the first conditional include:
  threatening   *You won't have any supper if you don't behave yourself!*
  bargaining   *If you cook, I'll clean.*
  offering   *I'll help if you want me to.*

FORMS

- Conditional sentences have at least two clauses – the *if* clause with the condition, and the main clause with the consequence.
- This is the standard form of the first conditional:
  If + present tense clause, + *will* clause
  If I see him   , *I'll give* him the books.
- Either the *if* clause or the consequence clause can come first. When the *if* clause comes second, there is usually no comma between the clauses.
  EXAMPLES: *If she **comes** now, we**'ll catch** the bus.*
  *We**'ll catch** the bus if she **comes** now.*

2 Second conditional sentences

USES

- We use the second conditional to talk about the consequences of present or future events that are possible but unlikely.
  EXAMPLE: *If you took an earlier train, we would/could meet you at the station.*
- The second conditional is also used to describe the consequences of a present or future situation which does not actually exist.
  EXAMPLE: *If I liked him, I would invite him.* (but I don't like him)
- The second conditional is often used to give advice.
  EXAMPLE: ***If I were you,*** *I would look for a better job.*

FORMS

- This is the standard form of the second conditional:
  If + past simple clause, + *would* clause
  If I told him   ,   he**'d be** angry.
- *Were* is often used instead of *was* in the first and third person singular, especially in formal English.
  EXAMPLE: *John would be much happier if he **were** married.*
- We can use other modals instead of *would* in the consequence clause.
  EXAMPLE: *If I told him, he **might/could** be angry.*
- As with the first conditional, either the *if* clause or the consequence clause can come first.
  EXAMPLE: *He**'d** be angry **if** I **told** him.*

3 *Should* and *ought to*

USE

- *Should* and *ought to* are used to give advice and to say what is a good idea or important to do.
  EXAMPLES: *You **shouldn't** worry so much. We **ought to** spend less on entertainment.*

FORMS

- *Should* is followed by an infinitive without *to*.
  EXAMPLE: *You **should see** a doctor.*
- *Ought* is followed by an infinitive with *to*.
  EXAMPLE: *You **ought to see** a doctor.*
- We form questions by putting *should* or *ought* before the subject.
  EXAMPLES: ***Should we** take him to the doctor? **Ought we to** take him to the doctor?*
  Note that it is unusual (and formal) to form a question with *ought*. Questions with *should* are much more common.
- We form the negative with *not/n't*.
  EXAMPLES: *We **should not/ shouldn't** stay here. We **ought not to/oughtn't to** stay here.*

FUNCTIONAL LANGUAGE

1 Giving advice
You should see a doctor.
You ought to think about it carefully.

2 Calming and reassuring someone
Don't worry/cry.
Don't be afraid.
It'll be all right.
Calm down.
Relax.

Talkback

Urban survival

John Wiseman, author of *The Urban Survival Handbook*, believes that everyone should carry a 'City Survival Kit' to help in any emergency. Look at some of the items he suggests.

Work in groups of four or five. One person should act as secretary and make notes.

1 In what situations would the items on the left be useful? Discuss different possibilities.
2 What else would you include in the kit and why? If you don't know what something is called in English, describe it to the others and see if they know.
3 When your list is finished, prepare to tell the class.
4 Discuss the lists other groups have made and agree on a final list of no more than fifteen items.
5 Ask your teacher for John Wiseman's original list. How does your list compare with his?

Needle and thread
- tie things together
- repair clothes
- cut things

4-ply pocket pack

Away from home

An unusual break

Focus

TOPIC
• Places to stay

GRAMMAR
• Defining relative clauses
• Relative pronouns: *who, which, that, whose*

SKILLS
• Reading: a magazine article
• Speaking: asking questions about vocabulary

GETTING STARTED

1 Look at these words for places where you can spend the night:

guesthouse   youth hostel
caravan park   campsite
self-catering flat   hotel
B & B (bed and breakfast accommodation)

1 Find places where:
   a) they serve you breakfast.
   b) you can get an evening meal.
   c) you can cook your own meals.
   d) you do not sleep in a building.

2 Which of these places do you think are:
   a) expensive?
   b) medium-priced?
   c) cheap?

3 Can you think of any more unusual places to spend a night?

READING

2 Before you read, look at the title of the article and the picture. What is the article about? List words that you think will be in the article, then compare your list with a partner's.

3 Now read the article to check your answers.

4 Answer these questions about the article.
1 Which part of the hotel is not made of snow?
2 What happens when winter ends?
3 What does every guest receive?
4 List all the unusual features of the hotel.

Cold comfort

Are you the kind of person who likes staying in unusual places? If the answer is 'yes', then try the world's coldest hotel in Jukkasjärvi in the north of Sweden. But go in winter or all you'll find is a pool of water, because the hotel melts every spring!

The man who runs the ARTic Hall Hotel is Nils Yngve Bergqvist. He is also the man whose idea it was.

He built his first igloo for an art exhibition in 1991 and he designed the present hotel – over 200 metres square – himself. It took workmen about two months to pile 1,000 tons of snow onto a wooden base. As the weather got colder, the snow froze and then they removed the base. The whole building and everything in it is made of snow – except for the

5 Now think about these questions.

1 Why is the hotel called the ARTic Hall Hotel?
2 Describe a typical room.
3 How might Nils Bergqvist describe his occupation?
4 Would you like to stay in the hotel? Why/why not?

wooden front door. There's a theatre which Nils uses for slide shows, a jazz club, a radio station and a large ice bar. As you can imagine, hot drinks are popular with the guests! The rooms have no doors, there's no furniture, no heating and everyone sleeps on ... yes, that's right ... ice beds. But the 800 people who have stayed at the hotel this winter seem to like it. If you want to stay in one of the ten ice rooms, it will cost you about £30 a night. You won't be very comfortable, but you will receive a survival certificate from the manager!

When the winter's over, Nils holds his annual contest to predict the day that the igloo will fall. The person that guessed the day correctly last year received a large painting from an ARTic Hall exhibition. Bergqvist's ice hotels are becoming world-famous and he loves his work. He's already excited about his next project – an ice hotel that will have more complicated architectural features and, he says, will be bigger and better.

DISCOVERING LANGUAGE

6 Look at these extracts from the article. The words in **bold** are defining relative clauses and the first word in bold each time is a relative pronoun.

A *The man **who runs the ARTic Hall Hotel** is Nils ...*
B *He is also the man **whose idea it was**.*
C *There's a theatre **which Nils uses for slide shows** ...*
D *The person **that guessed the day correctly** last year ...*
E *– an ice hotel **that will have more complicated architectural features**.*

1 Which relative pronouns refer to:
   a) a thing?   b) a person?
2 Are the statements below true or false?
   a) Relative pronouns are question words.
   b) A relative pronoun refers back to a noun or pronoun that comes before it.
   c) Relative clauses give more specific information about people or things.
3 Which relative pronoun is a less formal alternative to *which* or *who*?
4 Look at sentences F and G below. We need the relative pronoun in F, but not in G. What do you think the rule is?
   F *The paintings **that hang on the hotel walls** are for sale.*
   G *The paintings **(that) Nils hangs on the hotel walls** are for sale.*

7 Complete each sentence with a relative pronoun. In which sentences can you omit the relative pronoun?

1 There's a small town in Sweden ..... has an unusual hotel.
2 It's a hotel ..... is built from ice.
3 The man ..... built it is an artist.
4 It's a building ..... many people admire.
5 The hotel attracts visitors ..... idea of comfort is rather unusual.
6 There are many facilities ..... guests can use.
7 There are ten ice rooms ..... guests can choose from.

Would you like some ice?

SPEAKING

8 Work in pairs.

Student A: Look at the words below and ask questions to help your partner guess them.

butcher   receptionist   painter   passport   wardrobe   key

A: *What do you call a person who sells meat?*
B: *A person who sells meat is called a butcher.*

Student B: Turn to page 128. Answer your partner's questions. Then ask him/her to guess your words.

Continue the game by thinking of your own words.

Facilities

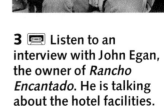

GETTING STARTED

1 Look at this list of hotel facilities:

a disco
tennis courts
fax machines
a swimming pool
a fast food snack bar
a high-quality restaurant
cartoon film shows
horse-riding
a room with a balcony
a room with a view
a sports centre

meeting rooms
tour guides
a children's playground
a babysitting service
secretarial services
mobile telephone hire
photocopiers
a laundry service
a dry-cleaning service
car hire
satellite television

1 Which facilities are important for:
a) a person on business?
b) a family with small children?
c) teenagers?
d) a young couple on holiday?
e) retired people?

2 Which facilities would *you* want to find in a hotel?

📱 Documentary

LISTENING

2 Before you listen, look at these pictures of *Rancho Encantado*, a ranch hotel in the United States. Why do you think people choose to stay at this hotel?

3 📼 Listen to an interview with John Egan, the owner of *Rancho Encantado*. He is talking about the hotel facilities.

1 In which part of the United States is the hotel?
2 What facilities does he mention?
3 What are these people responsible for?
a) the head wrangler
b) the recreation director

4 📼 Listen to the head wrangler, and then to John Egan again.

1 Are most guests experienced riders?
2 What are the two main reasons why people visit the area?

Focus

TOPIC
• Hotel facilities

GRAMMAR
• Causative: *have something done*

FUNCTIONS
• Polite requests
• Asking if something is possible
• Expressing satisfaction

SKILLS
• Listening: interviews, a hotel dialogue
• Speaking: discussion, role play

SPEECH PATTERNS
• Expressing satisfaction/ sarcasm

SPEAKING

5 What attracts you about a holiday at *Rancho Encantado*? What time of the year would you like to visit the hotel? Why?

DISCOVERING LANGUAGE

6 📼 Listen to this dialogue while you read it. What is the relationship between the two speakers? How do you know?

A: Hello, we've got a reservation. The name's Johnson.
B: Right, Mr Johnson. Let me see. Yes. Here we are. Two double rooms for three nights. Is that right?
A: Yes, that's it.
B: Would you mind filling in this form, please?
A: Sure. Is there a laundry service in the hotel?
B: Yes, sir. And we can have dry cleaning done for you too.
A: Excellent! Can I have my suit cleaned, then?
B: Certainly. I'll have it collected from your room.
A: Right. Er, … how long will it take?
B: You'll get the suit back this evening, sir.

1 Who is going to clean Mr Johnson's suit? A, B, or someone else?
2 Who is going to collect it from his room? A, B, or someone else?
3 Which verb pattern below expresses the two meanings in 1 and 2?
have + object + past participle
have + past participle + object
4 These sentences contain the same structure. Check your answer to 3. Explain when we use this structure.
I'll have the car washed today.
I need to have my bike mended.
Do you want to have your hair cut?
Have they had their order taken?

7 After a fire in a hotel, a lot of work was necessary to repair the rooms. Make sentences to describe the repairs.

the curtains/replace *They had the curtains replaced.*

1 the walls and ceilings/paint   4 the doors/mend
2 the carpets/clean   5 the pictures/change
3 the windows/repair   6 smoke alarms/fit

FOCUS ON FUNCTIONS

8 Look again at the dialogue in Exercise 6.

1 Find sentences that:
a) ask someone to do something.
b) ask if something is possible.
c) express satisfaction.
2 Which verb form follows *Would you mind … ?*
3 Make these requests more polite by using *Would you mind … ?*
a) Pay your bill now.   d) Show me your passport.
b) Sign this.   e) Please complete this questionnaire.
c) Let me see your card.

SPEECH PATTERNS

9 📼 Listen to two people using each of these phrases. Which speaker (A or B) is satisfied? What does the other speaker feel?

1 Excellent! *A*
2 Fantastic!
3 Wonderful!
4 Marvellous!
5 Oh, good.
6 It's very nice.
7 I've really enjoyed myself.
8 That's just what I wanted.
9 That's exactly what I'm looking for.

Listen again and repeat. How do we know when someone is being sarcastic?

SPEAKING

10 Work in pairs. Role play these conversations.

1 **Student A:** You are a guest in a hotel. You have returned to your room and found that the bed is unmade, the bathroom is dirty, and your laundry is still beside the door. Phone reception and ask for some action!
Student B: You are the receptionist. Respond to Student A.

2 **Student B:** You are the guest. You want lunch in your room. Phone room service and order some food and drink.
Student A: Answer the phone and take Student B's order. Then take the food and drink to the room. Make sure your partner signs the bill.

Telling stories

A

GETTING STARTED

1 Think about problems that you expect to experience if you visit a very different country from your own. Make a list and then show it to your partner. Which fears do you share? Which do you think are realistic?

Focus

TOPIC
• Experiences abroad

SKILLS
• Reading: a literary extract
• Listening: an anecdote
• Speaking: telling and retelling stories

READING: A LITERARY EXTRACT

2 The family of Gerald Durrell, a British naturalist, moved to a Greek island when he was a child. In his book *My Family and Other Animals* he describes how he found a scorpion in the garden with her babies on her back and put them all in a matchbox. Later, his brother Larry opened the box because he wanted to light a cigarette, and the scorpion climbed out.

1 What do you think happened next? Work in pairs and put the pictures in order.
2 Read the story and check the order of events.

3 Are these statements true or false? Correct the ones that are false.

1 Roger is a dog.
2 Leslie is a girl.
3 Margo threw a glass of water at the scorpion.
4 The water hit the dog.
5 The scorpion was killed.

4 Find these verbs in the text.

uttered   barking   scattering   thumped
sped (to speed)   quivering   leapt (to leap)
flicked   peered   hurled   drenched
swarmed

1 Which verbs refer to making a noise? What kind of noise, do you think?
2 Which verbs refer to movement from one place to another? What kind of movement?
3 Which verb means:
  a) jump?
  b) shake?
  c) throw something hard?
  d) look carefully?
  e) make a quick movement with your hand?
  f) make someone very wet?

C

Larry uttered a roar of fright that made Lugaretzia drop a plate and brought Roger out from beneath the table, barking wildly. With a flick of his hand he sent the unfortunate
5 - scorpion flying down the table, and she landed midway between Margo and Leslie, scattering babies like confetti as she thumped on the cloth. Thoroughly enraged at this treatment, the creature sped towards Leslie, her sting
10 - quivering with emotion. Leslie leapt to his feet, overturning his chair, and flicked out desperately with his napkin, sending the scorpion rolling across the cloth towards

SPEAKING

5 Work in pairs.
Student A: Look at the pictures and start to tell the story in your own words.
Student B: Look at the text and help your partner.

Change roles when you are about half-way through.

B

D

Margo, who promptly let out a scream that any
railway engine would have been proud to produce.   -15
Mother, completely bewildered by this sudden and
rapid change from peace to chaos, put on her glasses
and peered down the table to see what was causing
the pandemonium, and at that moment Margo, in a
vain attempt to stop the scorpion's advance, hurled a   -20
glass of water at it. The shower missed the animal
completely, but successfully drenched Mother, who
lost her breath and sat gasping at the end of the table,
unable even to protest. The scorpion had now gone
to ground under Leslie's plate, while her babies   -25
swarmed wildly all over the table.

6 What do you think happened next? Was
anyone hurt? What happened to the scorpions?
Did Gerald get into trouble?

LISTENING

7 📼 Listen to a holiday story and answer these
questions.

1 Which kind of holiday was it?
2 What did Willa do each night?
3 Why did they stay in one place for three days?
4 What was the problem with the campsite?
5 What did Willa find at the next campsite?

8 📼 Listen again and read the story. Compare it
with Durrell's written story.

1 What do you notice about the vocabulary?
2 How are the clauses joined together?
3 What other characteristics of conversational
English do you notice?

❝ The most interesting time was going to Ayers
Rock in Australia, and we were in … it was a
camping safari, so we were travelling around by
coach and they took all this amazing gear, and
every night we stopped and pitched camp – each
couple or group had to do their own tent … but
when we got to Ayers Rock, the coach had broken
down and we were stuck there for ages, for about
three days, and they'd had an infestation of mice –
a plague, literally a plague of mice. There were
mice everywhere, everywhere you looked. We
managed to keep, they managed to keep the camp
reasonably clear, the little campsite we were in,
and we left there, and the next day we moved on to
the next place and we pitched camp again and I
did the usual first thing – you know, sort of doing
the tent, and putting up the beds, the camp beds,
and getting the gear out. I unpacked my suitcase
and about six mice leapt out! ❞

9 Think of a story, real or imaginary, about
something that happened to you on holiday or in
another country. Consider these questions:

1 Where were you?
2 What were you doing there?
3 What happened?
4 How did you react?
5 What happened next?
6 How did it end?

SPEAKING

10 Work in pairs.

Student A: Ask your partner this question: *Has
anything strange ever happened to you on
holiday?* Listen to your partner's story and note
down the most important words. Ask questions if
you do not understand something or if you want
more information.

Student B: Tell your partner about your
experience.

**Then change roles. When you have finished, tell
the class your partner's story. Use your voice to
make it as interesting and dramatic as possible
for your listeners.**

Language reference

1 Defining relative clauses

There are two main types of relative clauses. In this book we look at defining relative clauses.

EXAMPLE: *Have you seen the hotel **that is made of ice?***

USE

Defining relative clauses give us more specific information about someone or something. This often helps to identify a person or thing.

EXAMPLE: *The country* [Which country?] ***that I like best*** *is Australia.*

FORMS

Defining relative clauses usually begin with a relative pronoun. In this unit, the relative pronouns are *who, which, that* and *whose.*

- *Who* refers to people, and is usually the subject of a relative clause.
  EXAMPLE: *Is she the woman **who interviewed you?***
- *Which* refers to things. It can be the subject or object of a relative clause.
  EXAMPLES: *It's a plan **which should work.** They're problems **which you have to solve.***
- *That* is used in defining relative clauses to refer to people or things. It can be the subject or the direct object of a clause. *That* is less formal than *who* or *which.*
  EXAMPLES: *He's the man **that works in the toy shop.** It's a bird **that I've never seen before.***
- *Whose* is the possessive relative pronoun.
  EXAMPLE: *He's the one **whose brother is an actor.***
- It is possible to omit the relative pronouns *that, who* and *which* when they are the *object* of the verb in the relative clause.
  EXAMPLES: *They're problems **(that/which) you have to solve.** She's the woman **(that/who) I interviewed.***

2 *Have something done*

USE

We use the structure *have something done* (causative) to stress that a job is the responsibility of someone else, not of the subject of the sentence. Note these contrasting examples:

*He**'s washing the car.*** (= He's washing it himself.)
*He**'s having the car washed.*** (= Someone is washing it for him.)

FORM

This structure is formed with *have/has* + object + past participle.
EXAMPLE: *I'd like to **have the house painted.***

FUNCTIONAL LANGUAGE

1 Making polite requests
   Would you mind signing here?

2 Asking if something is possible
   Can I have my suit cleaned?

3 Expressing satisfaction
   Excellent!

Progress check Units 6–7

GRAMMAR AND FUNCTIONS

1 Complete questions for these answers. Use first or second conditionals.

Where *would you stay if the youth hostel was full?*
If the youth hostel was full, I'd sleep on the beach.

1 What ..... ?
   If I failed my exams, I'd take them again.
2 When ..... ?
   If there are no seats on the 14th, we'll leave on the 15th.
3 How ..... ?
   If the coaches are full, he'll travel by car.
4 Where ..... ?
   If there weren't any local shops, I'd shop in the city.
5 How ..... ?
   If she needed a major operation, I'd feel frightened.

2 Fill each gap with *who, which* or *whose*. Then show which gaps can be left blank.

We've got a small house ^{1}..... we built ourselves just outside Lausanne. At the back of the house is Lake Geneva. In the summer the lake is full of boats ^{2}..... carry passengers ^{3}..... work or shop in other towns and villages. The house next door to ours is owned by a German couple ^{4}..... we see quite often. The people ^{5}..... house is immediately opposite ours have lived here for generations and are also friendly. There's a small shop ^{6}..... sells food and drink, but of course we go into Lausanne for things ^{7}..... we can't buy locally.

3 Change the sentences in the same way as the example, using the correct form of *have something done*.

They're taking their car to the car wash. (wash)
They're having their car washed.

1 A secretary typed the letters for her. (type)
2 A volunteer does his shopping for him. (do)
3 I'll ask someone to paint the fence. (paint)
4 They're going to the printers for some business cards. (print)
5 A photographer is going to take our picture. (take)

4 Write what you think, using both *should* and *ought to*.

Should I go to the dentist now or wait until my tooth hurts?
You shouldn't wait. You ought to go now.

1 Should students study all day or enjoy themselves?
2 Should people try to change their looks or accept them?
3 Should we have children at twenty or wait until we are thirty?
4 Should I talk about my fears or keep quiet?
5 Should we stay at the ice hotel or go somewhere hot?

5 Rewrite these sentences, keeping a similar meaning.

1 Can you get somebody to clean my suit?
   Can I ..... ?
2 Relax!
   Calm ..... !
3 Could you close the door, please?
   Would you mind ..... ?
4 I'm frightened of speaking in public.
   I'm very nervous .....

VOCABULARY

6 Use one word with either *-able* or *over-* to complete b) so that it has a similar meaning to a).

1 a) He looked too confident.
   b) He looked ..... .
2 a) Will they accept our conclusions?
   b) Will they find our conclusions ..... ?
3 a) Nobody can predict the results.
   b) The results are not ..... .
4 a) Be careful not to sleep too long.
   b) Be careful not to ..... .

8 *Paths to success*

Job options

Focus

TOPICS
- Jobs
- Qualifications
- School subjects

GRAMMAR
- Present perfect simple
- Adverbs: *for* and *since*

FUNCTIONS
- Talking about ambitions

SKILLS
- Reading: case studies

GETTING STARTED

1 Look at this list of jobs:

dentist	plumber	hotel receptionist
carpenter	postman	window dresser
cleaner	teacher	librarian
chef	firefighter	pharmacist
engineer	journalist	lorry driver
nurse	waiter	police officer

Divide the list into jobs that, in your country:

a) usually require university qualifications.
b) require qualifications but not at university level.
c) don't usually require qualifications.

Which of these jobs do you think you would be good or bad at? Why?

READING

2 Name the jobs in the pictures. Describe what each person is doing.

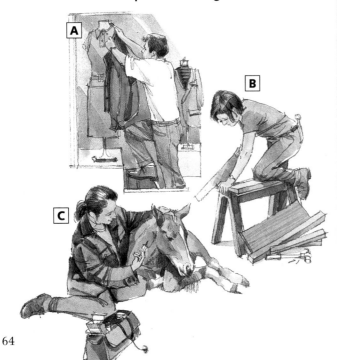

3 Now read about three young people and match them to the jobs in the pictures. What information surprises or interests you?

CAREER SPECIAL

1 Diana Stapleton, 28, has been a veterinary surgeon for three years. She has always loved animals. Now she works with three other vets and earns about £16,400 a year. Only six universities in Britain offer the five-year degree course to become a vet, and you need good 'A' level results in relevant subjects to get in. After graduating, vets can work with pets in cities or, like Diana, they can choose to have more contact with farm animals.

2 Paul Chambers, 22, is a senior window dresser at Selfridges, a department store in London. For £10,500 a year, his job is to make shop windows look so attractive that shoppers want to buy the goods. The thirty shop windows are changed once a month. A theme for the month is chosen and Paul is given some ideas. Paul completed a two-year course for a diploma in display design at a London college.

3 Two years ago Liz Cunningham joined a major building company as a youth trainee. Since then she has obtained a basic skills certificate in carpentry and at the age of twenty she now earns £10,600 a year. She is the only woman working in the building team. She recently began an advanced certificate course to learn more complex skills like roofing and making stairs. Her company pays for her to attend college once a week.

4 Which of the people in the texts:

a) have a qualification?
b) is still studying?
c) went to university?
d) can only work in a town?

5 Find words in the texts for particular qualifications.

a) a school qualification for university entrance
b) a university qualification
c) two qualifications from colleges

6 Which subjects do you think the three people liked best at school?

chemistry   biology   physics   religion   drama
mathematics (maths)   modern languages
English literature   geography   history   music
art   economics   craft, design and technology

Which subjects do/did you prefer? Give reasons for your answers.

↩ COMPARING CULTURES

7 In Britain, children start primary school at the age of five, and secondary school at eleven. Then, when they are sixteen, students take GCSE exams (General Certificate of Secondary Education) in up to ten subjects. Those who continue usually study three subjects at advanced level for two years before going on to higher education. About 14% then follow degree courses at college or university, which typically last for three years.

1 What ages do children in your country attend primary/secondary schools?
2 How many subjects do secondary students usually study in your country?
3 How long does it take to do a first degree course in your country?

FOCUS ON FUNCTIONS

8 📼 Listen to three different people talking.

1 Match them with the jobs in Exercise 2.
2 Listen again and complete these sentences about their ambitions:
   a) My . . . . . is to become a . . . . . .
   b) I . . . . . always . . . . . with animals.
   c) In the future, ... for myself.

9 Interview your partner about his/her ambitions. Use this language to help you:

Have you got any ambitions?/What would you like to do in the future?/Is there anything you've always wanted to do?
My ambition is to . . ./I'd like to . . ./I've always wanted to . . .

Now tell the class about your partner.

DISCOVERING LANGUAGE

10 Find examples in the texts opposite of statements with the present perfect.

1 Write an example of a negative statement and a question.
2 Which of these statements are true?
   The present perfect simple is used to refer to actions that:
   a) happened at a particular specified time in the past.
   b) happened at an unspecified time in the past.
   c) started in the past and continue now.
   d) started and ended in the past.
3 When do we use *for* and *since* with the present perfect? What is the difference in the way these two words are used?

11 Complete this imaginary interview with Liz Cunningham, using present perfect simple and past simple forms of the verbs in brackets.

INTERVIEWER: How long [1]. . . . . (you/be) a carpenter?
LIZ: [2]. . . . . about a year.
INT: [3]. . . . . (the company/employ) women before?
LIZ: No, it [4]. . . . . . At least, not as carpenters. I'm the first!
INT: [5]. . . . . (you/take) a carpentry course?
LIZ: Yes, I [6]. . . . . (finish) my basic skills course six months ago.
INT: [7]. . . . . (you/enjoy) the course?
LIZ: I [8]. . . . . (love) the course, but I [9]. . . . . (not use) all my new skills yet.

Focus

Preparing to work

▣ Documentary

LISTENING

1 Before you listen, look at the pictures of Katie Bunnell.

1 What do you think she does?
2 What is she making?
3 What qualifications do you think she already has?

2 ▣ Listen to an interview with Katie, and check your answers to Exercise 1. Then answer these questions.

1 Where is Katie studying?
2 How long is her course?
3 When did she start the course?
4 How long has she been at the college?
5 What does the final exam include?
6 When did she begin the 'legs' project?

3 ▣ Listen again. Complete this chart with nouns from the interview, and then add all the verbs that she uses with these nouns.

DEFINITION	NOUN IN INTERVIEW	RELATED VERB
a long piece of academic writing	. . . . .	. . . . .
a piece of work done over time that needs careful planning	. . . . .	. . . . .
a work of art made by shaping wood, clay, metal, stone, etc.	sculpture	make
a picture made by sticking various materials on to a surface	. . . . .	. . . . .

4 Which adjectives are used to describe:

a) an exam?   c) the colours of the legs?
b) Katie's 'legs'?   d) the background to the sculpture?

Guess the meanings of these words, and then check with your dictionary.

DISCOVERING LANGUAGE

5 Look at this sentence from the interview:

I've been studying for nearly two years.

1 How is the present perfect progressive formed?
2 Change the sentence so that it begins with: *she, you, we, they.*
3 Write a question that the sentence can answer: *How long ...*
4 Correct this sentence about Katie, using a negative: *She's been studying at Manchester University.*

6 Write questions and answers with the present perfect progressive.

learn/English? three years
How long have you been learning English? For three years.

1 study/economics? about a year   3 work/library? two o'clock
2 do/computer course? January   4 wait/interview? half an hour

DISCOVERING LANGUAGE

7 Think about the differences between simple and progressive forms.

1 Look at this pair of sentences. Which verb form tells us that the painting is definitely finished?
   A He's painted the living room.
   B He's been painting the living room.
2 Is there a difference in meaning between these two sentences?
   A I've worked all day.   B I've been working all day.

8 Use the simple or progressive forms to express these ideas.

1 You moved into this house in 1980, and still live there.
2 You started studying English in 1990.
3 You started your essay at 10.00 a.m. It's now 3.00 p.m. and you're still writing it.
4 You started playing tennis at 11.00 this morning. It's now 12.00 p.m. You've just finished your third game.

9 Read about Philip Hughes. Are the statements below true or false? Correct the false statements by changing the verb form.

1 Philip is a student.
2 He has been working as a lawyer for a week.
3 He worked on Brooklyn Bridge.
4 He has studied furniture design.
5 He has been mixing with other artists for some time.
6 He wears a suit.
7 He made furniture in a studio for a few years.
8 He has been living in London since he left New York.

DISCOVERING LANGUAGE

10 Note expressions in the article that refer to time sequence. *After ...*

Now complete this text with appropriate linking words and phrases.

My cousin studied anthropology. [1] .... she left university, she went to Fiji to do research for three years [2] .... returning to Canada. Two years [3] .... , in 1990, she went to India for a year, and [4] .... to Sri Lanka for another year. [5] .... she went back to Canada, she got a job teaching in a university and she's been there ever since.

WRITING

11 Write about your own or a friend's career. Use the outline to help you.

PARA. 1, background: *I'm a ... at ... I've been doing ... for ...*
PARA. 2, education and qualifications: *I went to ... school and got my secondary school certificate in history, geography, ... Then I went to ... university and left with a degree in ...*
PARA. 3, work experience: *My first job was ... Two years later ...*

I used to be a solicitor ...

After taking a degree at Sussex University, Philip put on a suit and became a lawyer. He remained a lawyer for less than a week and then took the suit off again. Eight years later, Hughes is happy with his life as a successful furniture designer because he's finally doing what he wants to do. When he left the legal profession, he got a job working on the Brooklyn Bridge in New York before returning to London and doing a course in furniture making. Then he won a place at the Royal College of Art to do a postgraduate course in design and spent time with artists and designers. Now he works in a studio that he shares with other artists and craft makers and makes furniture to his own designs.

Personal interviews

Focus

TOPIC
• Personal information

FUNCTIONS
• Asking for repetition
• Asking for clarification
• Correcting yourself
• Showing interest

SKILLS
• Reading: job advertisements
• Listening: a job interview
• Speaking: interviews

SPEECH PATTERNS
• Using intonation to introduce a new topic

READING

1 Read this job advertisement.

> **Live-in au pair** for two boys, four and six, in Hampstead area of London. Childcare and light housework. One year contract, renewable, £100 a week. Own room with television. Fare home paid at end of contract. Applicants should be 18–25 with good English and love of children. Driving licence essential. Phone 071-742 7700.

1 What is the job?
2 Where is it?
3 How old should applicants be?
4 Must applicants be British?
5 What is the pay?
6 Are there any other benefits?

LISTENING

2 A young man has applied for the job in Exercise 1. Before you listen, work with your partner and list the topics that the interviewer will want to ask about.

Education ...

3 🔲 Listen to the job interview. The interviewer covers seven 'topics'. Write the topic for each part.

1 Personal details
2 Reasons for being in Britain

4 🔲 Listen again and make notes on these questions.

1 Where is Emil from?
2 How old is he?
3 When did he come to Britain?
4 What has he been doing in Britain?
5 How many brothers and sisters has he got?
6 How old are they?
7 What does he do in Finland?
8 What is he studying?
9 How long has he been doing that?
10 What jobs has he done?
11 Has he worked with children before?

SPEECH PATTERNS

5 🔲 The interviewer uses these words when she moves to a new topic.

1 Does her voice go down (↘) or up (↗) at the end of each word?
So ...   Right ...   OK ...   Now ...

2 Listen and check your answers. Then practise saying the words.

6 🔲 Listen and read. Which of the four responses (a–d) sound:

1 interested and friendly?
2 uninterested and cold?

A: I've got a brother who lives in New York.
B: a) Really?   b) Oh.   c) Have you?
   d) New York?

Now listen and repeat these encouraging responses.

e) That's interesting.   i) How nice!
f) That's terrible!   j) How awful!
g) Do you?   k) I see.
h) How fantastic!   l) Oh, dear!

7 Work in pairs.

Student A: Read the sentences below.

Student B: Respond with an appropriate encouraging phrase.

Then change roles.

1 I won £1 million when I was young.
2 But then I lost it all.
3 I lost everything ... my house, my car.
4 Then I went to live in the States.
5 I made another fortune from computers.
6 Then I lost it all again.
7 So now I'm living here in the park.

FOCUS ON FUNCTIONS

8 📼 **Listen to the sentences below and match them to one of these functions:**

1 asking for repetition
2 asking for clarification
3 correcting yourself

a) Sorry?
b) Pardon?
c) Could you explain that?
d) Sorry, I mean ...
e) I'm afraid I don't understand.
f) Could you say that again?
g) Could you give me an example?

Listen again and repeat the phrases.

LISTENING

9 📼 **Look at the list of topics below.**

1 Which tenses did Emil use to talk about:
   a) his personal details?
   b) his family background?
   c) his education?
   d) his work experience?
   e) his hobbies?
2 Listen again to extracts from the conversation and check your answers.

SPEAKING

10 Work in groups of three.

Students A and B: You are going to have an interview for this job. Study the advertisement and make notes on questions you would like to ask about the job.

> ## COURIER WANTED *(July/August)*
>
> To accompany American children (11–14) and their teachers on a coach tour around Europe. The ideal candidate will be well travelled, patient and tolerant with a good sense of humour.
>
> Good spoken English essential; knowledge of other languages helpful. Candidates should be able to talk about European art, architecture, music and customs.
>
> *Phone 081-379 4406 for more details.*

Student C: You are the interviewer. Study the advertisement and then look at your notes below. Plan your questions.

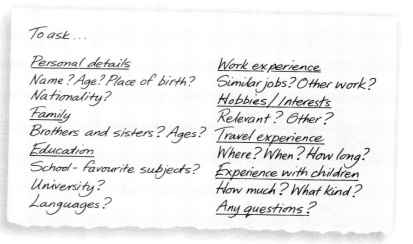

> To ask ...
>
> *Personal details*
> Name? Age? Place of birth?
> Nationality?
> *Family*
> Brothers and sisters? Ages?
> *Education*
> School – favourite subjects?
> University?
> Languages?
>
> *Work experience*
> Similar jobs? Other work?
> *Hobbies / Interests*
> Relevant? Other?
> *Travel experience*
> Where? When? How long?
> *Experience with children*
> How much? What kind?
> *Any questions?*

11 Work in the same groups of three.

Student A: You are the first candidate for the job advertised above. Use information about yourself, or your imagination, to help you answer the interviewer. At the end of the interview, ask questions about the job. Then listen to the second interview and make notes on any language problems.

Student B: Listen to the first interview and make notes on any language problems you notice. You are the second interviewee. Use information about yourself, or your imagination, to help you answer the interviewer.

Student C: You are the interviewer. Interview Student A and then Student B. Use the notes above to guide your questions. Invent answers to questions that candidates ask about the job.

Discuss which of the two candidates should get the job, and why. Then discuss language problems that were noted during the interviews.

Language reference

GRAMMAR

1 The present perfect simple

USES

We use the present perfect simple:

- to refer to something that happened in the past at an unspecified time.
  EXAMPLE: I**'ve been** to Greece.
- to refer to something that happened recently when the exact time is not important.
  EXAMPLE: The match **has finished**.
- to refer to a period of time from a point in the past continuing to the present moment.
  EXAMPLE: She **has been** here for ten years.
- to refer to a specific event that has not yet taken place.
  EXAMPLE: They **haven't interviewed** her yet.

FORMS

- The present perfect simple is formed from the auxiliary have + a past participle:
  Affirmative   I **have ('ve) seen** that film.
  Negative   I **have not (haven't) seen** that film.
  Question   **Have** you **seen** that film?
- Regular verbs form past participles by adding -ed to the infinitive.
- Some common irregular past participles in this book include:
  be – **been**   go – **gone**   do – **done**   have – **had**
  lose – **lost**   eat – **eaten**   meet – **met**
  come – **come**   become – **become**

2 For/since

These adverbs commonly occur with the present perfect.

- For refers to a period of time.
  EXAMPLE: I've been here **for half an hour**.
- Since refers to the particular point in time when the action or situation began.
  EXAMPLE: I've been here **since last Saturday**.

3 The present perfect progressive

USES

We use the present perfect progressive:

- to refer to a period of time continuing from a point in the past to the present moment, or to the very recent past.
  EXAMPLE: She**'s been training** for two years.
- to emphasise the continuity of an action or situation.
  EXAMPLE: I**'ve been having** fun.

Some verbs have a sense of continuity in their basic meaning (e.g. live, work, wait, stay, drive, walk, listen).There is little or no difference in meaning between the simple and progressive forms of the present perfect when these verbs are followed by for or since.

EXAMPLES:

He**'s walked** to work for as long as I can remember.
He**'s been walking** to work for as long as I can remember.

- to emphasise the repetition of a quick action in a period that continues to the present.
  EXAMPLE: We**'ve been knocking** on the front door.

FORMS

- The present perfect progressive is formed from the auxiliary have + been + an -ing verb form.
  Affirmative   He **has ('s) been living** here for ten years.
  Negative   He **has not (hasn't) been living** here for long.
  Question   **Has** he **been living** here for a long time?
- The progressive form of the present perfect is not normally used with:
  stative verbs (e.g. be, like, know, want, understand).
  verbs that refer to quick, single actions (e.g. land, take off, start, stop), but see the last point under USES above.

FUNCTIONAL LANGUAGE

1 Talking about ambitions
My ambition is to be a sculptor.
I'd like to become a lawyer.
I've always wanted to manage a company.

2 Asking for repetition
Sorry?
Pardon?
Could you say that again?

3 Asking for clarification
Could you explain that?
I'm afraid I don't understand.
Could you give me an example?

4 Correcting yourself
Sorry, I mean I <u>used</u> to work in advertising.

Talkback

Happy endings

Work in groups of three.

1 Look at the pictures and describe what you see in each one. What are the possible relationships between the three main characters? Where are they in each scene?

2 You can order the pictures in a number of different ways. Discuss all the possibilities and then choose the one you prefer. Imagine what happens between the scenes shown in the pictures.

3 Give the characters names and tell the story in the sequence you prefer. Use present tenses (including the present perfect) to tell the story.

4 Decide what the people are saying to each other in each scene, and write a script. Use this convention for writing scripts:
Liz: [angrily] Why ... ?

5 Act out your story to the rest of the class.

9 *Skin deep*

Focus

TOPIC
• People's appearances

GRAMMAR
• *Look* + adjective
• *Look like* + noun

FUNCTIONS
• Certainty and probability in the future

SKILLS
• Listening: a discussion
• Speaking: a discussion
• Writing: a short report

VOCABULARY DEVELOPMENT
• Adjectives describing people

First impressions

GETTING STARTED

1 Look at the man in Picture A.

1 How old do you think he is?
2 What do you think he does?
3 Describe the picture.

2 📼 Two people are talking about the man in the picture. Do they recognise him? How do you know?

DISCOVERING LANGUAGE

3 Study the use of *look* in these sentences from the dialogue.

A *He looks awful.*
B *He looks nice.*
C *He looks middle-aged.*
D *He looks like an old tramp.*

1 Which phrase describes:
   a) age? b) appearance?
   c) personality?
2 Which parts of speech follow each of these constructions?
   a) He looks …   b) He looks like …

DEVELOPING VOCABULARY

4 Pictures B and C are of the same person as Picture A. Look at all three pictures.

1 How old do you think he is in each picture?
   He looks about …   He's probably about …
2 The words below describe *appearance*. Match them to the three pictures.
   clean   dirty   smart   scruffy   young
   old   drab   colourful   old-fashioned
   fashionable   clean-shaven   unshaven
   In Picture B he looks smart, but his clothes look old-fashioned.
3 Use these words to make judgements about the man's *personality*:
   innocent   mature   immature   relaxed
   intelligent   rebellious   forgetful
   serious   crazy   interesting   aggressive
   conventional   unconventional   dull
   poor   rich   boring   fun-loving
   unintelligent
   I think he looks very immature in Picture C.
4 Compare the man with other types of people that you know.
   He looks like an ordinary schoolboy.
5 Describe the changes he has made to his appearance between Pictures B and C.
   He's changed his hair style.

↻ COMPARING CULTURES

5 The pictures opposite are of Nigel Kennedy, an internationally known British violinist. Most people – performers and audience – wear smart clothes to certain events like classical concerts, the opera, and the ballet. How do people in your country dress when they attend or perform in a concert?

What kind of events do you attend in smart clothes?

LISTENING

6 Before you listen, use expressions from this list to describe the appearance of the people below.

The man's had his hair dyed.

have your hair dyed/cut
grow your hair/a beard/your nails
have your head shaved
have your arm tattooed
buy a wig
have your ear pierced
have cosmetic surgery
have your nose pierced
have your teeth straightened

Work in pairs. Discuss other ways of changing your appearance. Have you made any changes recently?

7 📼 Three women are discussing changes to their appearance. Listen to the first part.

1   Which person (Lucy, Pam or Jenny):
 a) thinks she will dye her hair?
 b) is sure she will dye her hair?
 c) doesn't think she will dye her hair?
2   Listen to the second part of the conversation and name the person who:
 a) has decided to have a tattoo.
 b) thinks there is a small possibility that she will have a tattoo.
 c) is sure she will not have a tattoo.
3   Do the women know each other? How do you know?
4   How old do you think Lucy is? What makes you think that?

FOCUS ON FUNCTIONS

8 📼 Listen again. Find the expressions on the right which mean:

1   I'm certain (I will).   a) I think …
2   There's a strong chance   b) I'm sure …
     (that I will/won't).   c) It's possible …
3   There's a small   d) I'll definitely …
     possibility (that I will/   e) I'm not sure …
     won't).   f) I probably won't …
                                             g) I'll probably …

9 Would you change your appearance? Work in groups. Discuss changes like the ones in Exercise 6. Ask one student in the group to complete a chart like this:

WOULD YOU …	DYE YOUR HAIR?	HAVE YOUR HEAD SHAVED?
definitely	Anne	
probably	Elsa	
possibly	Jordi	
definitely not	Gregor	

WRITING

10 Read the text below and then write a similar text about your group.

Anne would dye her hair. In fact, she has already dyed her hair a few times. Gregor definitely wouldn't because he thinks men look stupid with dyed hair. Elsa thinks she will probably dye her hair when she's older – especially if she starts going grey. Jordi doesn't really know. He doesn't think he will at the moment but it's possible in the future.

A professional interest

🎧 Documentary

Focus

TOPIC
• Models and model agencies

GRAMMAR
• *Must, can't, might, could* + *be*

FUNCTIONS
• Guessing
• Making deductions

SKILLS
• Listening: a monologue, sound sequences

SPEECH PATTERNS
• Running words together

LISTENING

1 Before you listen, look at the pictures.

1 What is the purpose of the card? Who is it given to? Who gives it?
2 What do you think the two women's jobs are?
3 What qualities do you think a successful model needs? Think about looks and personality.

2 Match the expressions and the definitions below. Use a dictionary to help you.

1 a scouting programme
2 a would-be model
3 a bona fide agency
4 an open-door policy
5 a portfolio
6 shots
7 symmetrical features
8 a good profile

a) photographs
b) a real and honest business
c) an attractive side view of a face
d) a collection of pictures
e) a system without appointments
f) a plan for finding people
g) a person who wants to be a model
h) regular characteristics of a face

Use these phrases to say how you think people become models.

3 📼 Chris Owen is a director of the Elite Premier model agency in London, which finds models (mainly women) for advertisers, magazines and fashion designers. The people from the agency who find the models are called *bookers*. Listen to part of an interview with Chris Owen.

1 How does the agency find new models? Were your guesses in Exercise 2 correct?
2 What does the agency look for in new models?

4 📼 Listen to the second part of the interview and say which of these people the information below describes:

Susie   Cathy   Joanna

a) She's half-Chilean.
b) They're English.
c) They look Spanish or Italian.
d) She used to work in a shoe shop.
e) She was in a modelling competition.
f) She is a top English model.

Which picture at the top of the page shows Cathy?

5 📼 **Listen to the first part of the interview again and say what you think.**

1 Do you think Elite Premier is a good agency? Why/why not?
2 What do you think a really bad agency is like?
3 Chris Owen says that good models must have 'great personalities' and 'professional attitudes'. What do you think he means by these?
4 Does anyone in your class match Chris Owen's idea of a model?

FOCUS ON FUNCTIONS

6 **Look at Picture A and say where you think the women are from. Then read this dialogue. Do you agree?**

A: They look Middle Eastern to me.
B: Yes, they could be, but I don't think so. I suppose they might be African.
A: Well, they can't be from southern Africa. Their skins are too pale.
B: Well, then they must be from one of the desert countries like Mali or Niger.

7 **Look back at the dialogue in Exercise 6.**

1 Find four verb phrases used to make a guess or a deduction.
2 Complete a chart like this with the phrases:

POSSIBLE	CERTAIN (+)	CERTAIN (-)

8 **Look at Picture B and complete the conversation below with:**

must be   can't be   might be   could be

A: What's that animal skin?
B: It ¹..... a horse. Look at the horns! It ²..... a reindeer, but I'm not sure.
A: If it *is*, the man ³..... from Scandinavia – from Lapland. He certainly looks cold.
B: Yes, I agree. Do you think those are his normal clothes?
A: I don't know. Perhaps – or this ⁴..... a special occasion.

SPEECH PATTERNS

9 📼 **In fluent speech, the endings of words often change, depending on the word that follows. Listen to these sentences. What happens to the end of the first underlined word in each case?**

a) She <u>must be</u> quite old.   c) He <u>might be</u> Chinese.
b) They <u>could be</u> friends.   d) They <u>can't be</u> in France.

Now listen again and repeat.

10 📼 **Listen to three groups of sounds. Each group contains several sounds.**

1 Listen to the first sound. Guess where the place is.
2 Listen to the second sound and guess again.
3 Listen to the other sounds and identify the place.

Use these phrases to help you:

It might be ...   It could be ...   Perhaps it's ...   I've got no idea.
It can't be ...   It must be ...   It's definitely ...   I'm quite sure it's ...
You're probably right.   I think so too.

Describing appearances

Focus

TOPICS
- Unusual models
- Ordinary people
- Ideas of beauty

SKILLS
- Reading: an article
- Writing: descriptions of people

VOCABULARY DEVELOPMENT
- Compound adjectives and prepositional phrases

A

B

C

D

E

F

Model Models

Is there a place for a modelling agency that specialises in models who look ordinary, or even ugly? Jill Searle knows there is because she has been running the UGLY model agency in London since 1969.

READING

1 Before you read, look at the pictures.

1 Which people in the pictures do you think are professional models? Explain your choice.
2 Which ones can you imagine seeing in advertisements? What products could they advertise?
3 Read the title of the article above. What do you think it is about?
4 Which of the people in the pictures do you think the article refers to?

2 Read the article and check your answers to question 3 in Exercise 1.

3 Which of these statements are true according to the article? Correct the ones that are not true.

1 All models must be good-looking.
2 There is a demand for ordinary-looking people in fashion modelling.
3 Ugly men do not get a lot of work.
4 Advertising agencies do not like hiring ugly women.
5 There are no agencies like UGLY in the United States.

⟳ COMPARING CULTURES

4 Work in pairs and discuss these questions.

1 Do you think it is true that American films set standards of physical beauty all over the world? What are these Hollywood ideas of beauty?
2 Are ideas of beauty different in different countries? Are there ideas of beauty in your country that are different from those of Hollywood? What are the differences?

Her idea was to provide models who looked like 'real' people. In the world of fashion modelling, ordinary people
5- look out of place. They're not slim and beautiful with perfect skin and teeth; they're too short, too tall, too fat, too thin, or, they just look a bit …
10- dull. But according to Jill Searle, there is plenty of other modelling work outside the fashion world. She has some very unusual-looking people
15- on her books, but it is the ordinary-looking people who are in demand by advertisers.

The strange thing is that ugly women are not so much
20- in demand, whereas ugly men seem to be more acceptable. 'When we began we signed up all sorts of strange-looking females, but we found they couldn't get any work in
-25 advertising. If a TV commercial needs a woman with broken teeth, they prefer to make her look ugly with make-up – society does not
-30 seem to like the real thing and advertising agencies appear to feel that ugly women are just too risky.'

The whole world is
-35 affected by Hollywood's ideas of physical beauty, but even in the land of Californian sun-bleached blondes and well-oiled, muscle-bound Rambos
-40 there is an agency offering models that look like real people.

'All we want to do is offer a range of physical types – there
-45 is work for most of them.'

DEVELOPING VOCABULARY

5 Complete a chart like the one below.

1 Look through the article again and find words and phrases that the writer uses to contrast 'real' people with fashion models.

	ONE-WORD ADJECTIVES	COMPOUND ADJECTIVES	PREPOSITIONAL PHRASES
Real people and UGLY models	short	ordinary-looking	with broken teeth
Fashion models	…..	…..	…..

2 Work in pairs and use a dictionary to help you. Think of other words and phrases that can be used to describe ordinary people and fashion models. Here are a few examples:

	ORDINARY PEOPLE	FASHION MODELS
One-word adjectives	overweight	fit
Compound adjectives:		
a) adjective + noun + *ed*	bald-headed	…..
b) adjective + present participle	…..	good-looking
c) adverb + past participle	…..	well-built
Prepositional phrases	with hairy hands	with olive skin

WRITING

6 Work in pairs.

1 Look at the simple sentences below and picture each person and situation in your mind. Discuss your imaginary pictures, choose one and add descriptive words and phrases to the sentence to complete the description.
   a) A man stood on the platform.
      A bright-eyed young man with long blond hair stood impatiently on the crowded platform.
   b) A woman ran through the city centre.
   c) A small boy played in the park.

2 Now discuss the personality and state of mind of each person, and add a second sentence to each description.
   a) *He looked unhappy./He looked like a man who was always in a hurry.*

3 Add a third sentence to each description. Explain the true situation.
   In fact, he was usually a calm person who accepted life as it came, but today he was worried about his job and he did not want to be late for work.

4 Show your three-sentence description to a different partner and discuss how you could improve or add to it.

5 Now write a descriptive paragraph about someone you have seen today. Use present tenses to describe the person as you see them in your mind and then use your imagination to deduce the person's true situation.

7 After writing, exchange texts with another pair of students and try to improve each other's work. Then read your texts to the class.

Language reference

GRAMMAR

1 Look/look like

USES

- Like other sense verbs (e.g. *smell, taste, feel, sound*), the verb *look* can have different meanings. We can use it with the meaning of directing our eyes towards something.
  EXAMPLE: **Look** at this picture!

- We can also use it to describe characteristics of people or things.
  EXAMPLES: He **looks** terrible. She**'s looking** much older these days.

FORMS

- When *look* is used to describe characteristics, it is followed by an adjective, *not* an adverb.
  EXAMPLE: The food **looks delicious**.

- We can use phrases with numbers after *look* to talk about the age that a person or thing appears to be.
  EXAMPLES: She **looks about ten**. The dress **looks a hundred years old**.

- *Look* can also be followed by *like* + noun phrase. Note the two possible meanings of *look like* in this sentence.
  He **looks like** a tramp. =
  a) he has the appearance of a tramp, so he probably is one.
  b) he has the appearance of a tramp, but it is only a similarity.

2 Must, could, might, can't

USES

- In this unit, these modal verbs are used to refer to the probability of something, based on the evidence that the speaker has.
  EXAMPLE: She **can't be** a professional model because she hasn't got an agent.

- We use *must be* when we believe something is true, and *can't be* when we believe something is not. We use *could be* and *might be* to express the possibility that something is true.
  EXAMPLES: He **can't be** Australian, because his English isn't very good. He **could/might be** Malaysian. He **must be** Indonesian, because he's just arrived from Jakarta.

- We use certain common phrases with *can't be* and *must be* when we are angry or surprised.
  EXAMPLES: You **can't be** serious! You **must be** mad!

FORMS

- In these senses the modals are often followed by the verb *to be* and a noun phrase or an adjective.
  EXAMPLES: She **might be John's sister**. He **must be lazy**.

- Other structures are also possible.
  EXAMPLE: They **might be lying**.

FUNCTIONAL LANGUAGE

1 Talking about definite future events
I'm certain/sure (that) I'll dye my hair.
I'll definitely have my teeth straightened.

2 Talking about probable future events
There's a strong chance (that) I'll have cosmetic surgery.
I'll probably buy a blond wig.

3 Talking about possible future events
There's a small possibility (that) he'll have his head shaved.
It's possible (that) he'll grow a beard.
She's not sure if she'll have her hair dyed.

4 Making deductions
They must be very rich.
That can't be their house.

5 Making guesses
He could be a pop star.
He might be an actor.
Perhaps he's a model.

Progress check Units 8–9

1 Complete these sentences with the correct form of *look* or *look like*.

1 She ..... about twenty-five.
2 She ..... a musician – or an actress, perhaps.
3 I think she ..... interesting.
4 She ..... my sister.
5 She thinks she ..... attractive.
6 Her clothes (not) ..... old-fashioned.

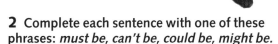

2 Complete each sentence with one of these phrases: *must be, can't be, could be, might be.*

1 She speaks with a New York accent, so she ..... from the USA.
2 She ..... a dancer, but I don't think so. She's not really tall enough.
3 She ..... a painter. I know some of her friends are.
4 She lives in a tiny flat so she ..... very rich.

3 Fill each gap with a present perfect simple or progressive form of the verb in brackets, or choose either *for* or *since*.

Adelle Wainwright [1]..... (live) in London [2]..... the last year. She [3]..... (try) to make a career in the theatre and [4]..... (already/have) some parts in small productions. 'It's been quite difficult but I [5]..... (be) lucky. I was in a play at the Almeida Theatre for a few months, but that [6]..... (finish) now. I had nothing [7]..... a few months but then I got a part in a television series and I [8]..... (do) that [9]..... February. I'd love to work in films but I [10]..... (achieve) that ambition yet!' [11]..... she came to Britain, Adelle [12]..... (learn) to play the violin. 'I'm not very good but I enjoy playing so much.'

4 Answer this question in three ways by continuing the sentences below: *What would Adelle like to do in the future?*

1 She'd like ...
2 She's always ...
3 Her ambition ...

5 Respond to each question in two ways. Use expressions from the list that show the same degree of certainty.

Are you sure? *Yes, I'm certain. Definitely.*

1 So you're not certain? *No, ...*
2 So there's a good chance that you'll go? *Yes, ...*
3 So perhaps we can get the next train? *Yes, ...*

maybe   it's possible   I'm not sure
almost certainly   it's not definite
I'm certain   definitely   probably

6 Imagine you are the woman from Unit 8 who was interviewing people to look after her children and live in her house. Put these adjectives describing appearance into three groups, from the woman's point of view.

a) positive adjectives
b) negative adjectives
c) neutral adjectives

clean   dirty   scruffy   immature   crazy
interesting   aggressive   boring
clean-shaven   serious   forgetful   smart
fit   bald-headed   unshaven   good-looking
old-fashioned   relaxed   rebellious
fun-loving   rich   untidy   sensitive

10 | *Showtime*

Story-telling

Focus

TOPIC
• Puppets

GRAMMAR
• *Be able* + *to* + infinitive
• *Manage* + *to* + infinitive

FUNCTIONS
• Talking about achievement

SKILLS
• Reading: an informative text
• Speaking: considering possibilities

VOCABULARY DEVELOPMENT
• Related words

✪ COMPARING CULTURES

1 Look at the pictures.

1 What can you see? What are the objects for? What do you think they are made of?

2 Are these traditional in your country? What are they made of in your country? Are they used to tell special stories?

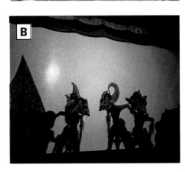

READING

2 Read the text below and check your answers to question 1 above. Say which country the puppets in the pictures are from, and name some of them.

Story-telling through puppets

In most parts of the world, as far back as anyone can remember, there has been a puppet tradition. Although some of us think of puppets as children's entertainment, they were – and often still are – used to tell serious stories to adult audiences. Even in these days of sophisticated film animation and special effects, the puppet theatre still has a special place in many cultures and no doubt people will be able to see the traditional characters for many more years.

The best-known puppet characters in Britain are Punch and Judy, glove puppets with wooden heads. In the summer, one basic play of about half an hour is performed, with variations, on beaches all around Britain. Mr Punch, who has an enormous nose and wears a curved hat, gets into trouble and has arguments with his wife, Judy. There is the baby, Toby the dog, a policeman, a crocodile, and a hangman, and all of them chase Mr Punch. He, of course, invariably manages to survive to fight another day.

In Belgium wooden puppets, or marionettes, first appeared in the 1820s in cities like Liège. The Liège puppets are in fact string puppets without strings! They have a single metal rod attached to their heads, which means the puppeteers aren't able to raise the arms and legs, but can move the body up and down and the head from side to side. Many of the stories used to be historical or religious but it is Tchantchès, a comic character with patched trousers and a big black hat, who is the best-loved character today. Like Mr Punch, he is a simple man who is also greedy, quarrelsome and lazy. He makes fun of everyone, but is often warm-hearted and tender.

In *wayang kulit*, the shadow puppet theatre of Java, two-dimensional leather puppets, operated from below by sticks, are moved around behind an illuminated cotton screen. This type of theatre can also be found in other parts of south-east and central Asia. The stories are usually based on Hindu epics, and a traditional performance can last all night. The characters in these stories are brought to life by the *dalang*, who is a very special kind of person. He sits in the same place all night, manipulating dozens of puppets on his own. He manages to tell a long and complex story without a script, while also controlling the orchestra.

3 Now answer these questions about the text.

1 Which of the puppets are controlled:
   a) from above?
   b) from below?
2 How long are the Punch and Judy and the *wayang kulit* shows?
3 Which characters make audiences laugh?
4 Which form of puppetry do you think is the most skilful? Why?

4 Find adjectives in the third paragraph which show that Tchantchès:

1 dislikes work.
2 wants a lot of everything.
3 is not very intelligent.
4 is kind.
5 often starts arguments.
6 is gentle and loving.

Use a dictionary to help you check your answers.

DEVELOPING VOCABULARY

5 Find related words in the text to complete these charts.

NOUN	ADJECTIVE
tradition	.....
wood	.....
basis	.....
comedy	.....
quarrel	.....
history	.....
religion	.....

VERB	NOUN
entertain	.....
vary	.....
argue	.....
perform	.....

DISCOVERING LANGUAGE

6 Look at these extracts from the text:

A ... the puppeteers **aren't able** to raise the arms and legs, ...
B ... people **will be able** to see the traditional characters for many more years.
C He **manages** to tell a long and complex story without a script, ...

1 Which of these modal verbs best expresses the meaning of *is able*?
   a) has to   b) should   c) can
2 What part of speech follows the verb forms in **bold**?
3 Change Extract A into an affirmative statement.
4 Change Extract B into a question and then a negative statement.
5 *Manage* is a regular verb. Change Extract C into a question and then a negative statement.
6 Which of these two sentences suggests a more difficult problem?
   She was able to solve the problem.
   She managed to solve the problem.
   Can you make a rule about the use of *manage*?

7 Complete the sentences with the correct form of *be able* or *manage*.

1 We ..... to follow the story although we couldn't understand the words. You speak Javanese, don't you? So presumably you ..... to understand it. I don't know how a *dalang* ..... to remember such a long story.
2 The Punch and Judy show starts at four p.m. ..... you ..... to stay until then? We ..... to have any lunch at the hotel, so I'm going to buy some snacks before it begins.
3 The museum was closing but we ..... to persuade the guard to show us the puppets. We ..... to see the rest of the museum, though, so we'll go back tomorrow.

SPEAKING

8 Work in pairs. You are going out for the day but you have to look after a boy of seven. Discuss where to go and the advantages and disadvantages of each place for all of you. Possible places to go include: the shops, the cinema, the beach, a park, a funfair, a swimming pool, the zoo.

A: *We could go to an amusement arcade.*
B: *No, he's too young. We won't be able to take him in.*
A: *But we'll be able to go in. He can wait outside!*

Focus

Stages

GETTING STARTED

1 Discuss these questions in pairs.

1 Do you ever go to the theatre? What kind of shows do you prefer?
modern plays   musicals   opera
comedies   ballet   classical plays

2 Identify these parts of a theatre in Picture A: stage   curtain   stalls
box   dress circle   upper circle

3 What do you think the people in Picture B are talking about? Make a list of words and phrases they might use.

🎬 Documentary

LISTENING

2 🔊 Listen to Andrew Leigh, Manager of the Old Vic theatre in London.

Part 1
1 Why is the Old Vic special?
2 When was it built?
3 Where did its name come from?

Part 2
4 How many theatres are there in London?
5 What influences have helped to change theatre styles recently?
6 In Andrew Leigh's opinion, will live theatre survive in Britain?

3 🔊 Listen to a conversation at the theatre box office.

1 Look at your list of phrases from question 3 in Exercise 1. Were you right?
2 Which evening does the customer want tickets for?
3 How many tickets does she buy?
4 Which part of the theatre are the seats in?
5 What are the seat numbers?
6 How much is each ticket?
7 When does the performance start?

4 🔊 Listen again and write down what the people say when they:

a) offer help.
b) ask for tickets.
c) ask about the number of tickets.
d) agree to take the tickets.
e) give the time of the performance.

Suggest other ways of saying these.

a) (offering help) *Yes, madam?
What can I do for you?*

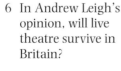

5 📻 Listen to a similar but *impolite* conversation at another theatre. How is this conversation different from the last one?

SPEAKING

6 Work in pairs.

Student A: You are the customer. You want three tickets for a performance of *Macbeth* one evening next week. Use your imagination to answer questions.

Student B: You work at the theatre box office. Turn to page 128 for the information you need. Be polite with your customer.

FOCUS ON FUNCTIONS

7 Consider the different uses of *can* and *could*.

1 Match the sentences with the functions.
   a) My brother, the actor, can learn lines quickly. — REQUEST
   b) I'm sorry. I can't meet you after work. — ABILITY
   c) She's under eighteen so she can't see the film. — PROHIBITION
   d) Can I have two tickets, please? — PERMISSION
   e) At eighteen we can see any film at the cinema. — DEDUCTION
   f) That man? He can't be a famous actor. — POSSIBILITY

2 Rewrite the sentences above with *could/couldn't*. Which ones still have the same function? Which are now in the past?

8 *Be able* is also used to talk about natural or learned ability and possibility. Study the table below. It shows two differences between *can* or *could* and *be able*. What are those differences?

		PRESENT	FUTURE	PAST
ABILITY (e.g. speak Chinese)		can am/is/are able	— will be able	could was/were able
POSSIBILITY (e.g. buy tickets)	general	can am/is/are able	can will be able	could was/were able
	on a single occasion	can am/is/are able	can will be able	couldn't (not could) was/were able

9 Identify the functions of the sentences below. Then discuss alternative ways of completing the sentences with forms of *can*, *could* and *be able + to*.

1 We arrived at the theatre late, so we . . . . . get tickets.
2 Both my sisters . . . . . speak a foreign language by the age of ten.
3 'Sorry, boys. Only adults . . . . . attend this performance.'
4 I . . . . . use all the computer functions after the course ends.
5 When I was young I . . . . . go to school on foot because it was too far.
6 The bus was late but she . . . . . get to the theatre in time.
7 . . . . . you give me a lift home after the play's finished?
8 We . . . . . get tickets for the Nirvana concert last Saturday.

READING: A LITERARY EXTRACT

10 Read this short extract from a famous speech in *As You Like It*, a play by William Shakespeare.

All the world's a stage

And all the men and women merely players:

They have their exits and their entrances;

And one man in his time plays many parts,

His acts being seven ages.

William Shakespeare (1564–1616) was an English dramatist and poet. Many of his plays, both tragedies and comedies, are well known throughout the world. They include *Hamlet, King Lear, Macbeth, A Midsummer Night's Dream, Romeo and Juliet* and *The Merchant of Venice*. The Globe Theatre, where many of his plays were originally performed, has recently been reconstructed in London.

1 What comparison is Shakespeare making? Do you think the comparison is a good one? Say why/why not.
2 Who do you think the words *man* and *his* refer to?
3 Use your own words to explain what Shakespeare meant. *The whole world is like a stage . . .*
4 The seven ages refer to seven periods in a person's life. Here are two that Shakespeare refers to in the rest of the speech. What do you think the others are? *the infant, the schoolchild, . . .*

Focus

TOPICS
- Circuses
- Animal performers

FUNCTIONS
- Giving opinions

SKILLS
- Reading: an article, a letter
- Listening: monologues
- Speaking: discussion
- Writing: a letter

VOCABULARY DEVELOPMENT
- Negative prefixes

SPEECH PATTERNS
- Using stress to show disagreement

Unnatural acts?

At a circus in Moscow, Walter Zapashny enters a cage with no fewer than four lions, nine tigers, two black panthers, a leopard and a puma. He feeds a lion from
5- his mouth and rides on the back of another.

Zapashny has worked in the circus since he was six. His family has been in the business for over a century. 'I dreamed of working with animals all my life. I wanted
10- to tame all kinds, including sea animals – seals, dolphins, sharks. Unfortunately, the conditions I was offered for working with these were not good.'

So he decided to work with big cats
15- instead, and it took him three years to get his first show together. Then he was mauled by a tiger and suffered 64 wounds. 'Every day I come to work, I tell myself what I do is dangerous.'
20- Zapashny took me to see the animals waiting for the evening's performance. They were in steel cages on wheels, so small that the animals had difficulty turning round. Walter put his hand into one cage and
25- tickled a lion under the chin.

Did he think the animals were treated properly? 'I am not satisfied. I love them and would like to have a park for them. They live longer than they do in the wild, but their
30- conditions are not natural.'

Giving opinions

GETTING STARTED

1 Circuses are traditional entertainment in many parts of the world.

1 Look at this list of circus performers:
  acrobats   lion tamers
  fire eaters   clowns
  human cannonballs
  ringmasters
  Which performers:
  a) introduce the acts?
  b) make people laugh?
  c) do dangerous stunts?

2 Which of these animals do you expect to see at a circus?
  horses   monkeys
  big cats   camels
  elephants   mice
  sea animals   bears

READING

2 Before you read, look at the picture of Walter Zapashny, a circus performer, and discuss these questions.

1 Why do you think he works with animals?
2 Is it a dangerous job?
3 In what conditions do you think he keeps his animals?
4 Do animals live longer in a circus or in the wild?
5 Why do you think the writer has used the title 'Unnatural Acts'?

3 Read the article and check your answers to the questions in Exercise 2.

4 Find these words in the article.

1 The names for:
   a) five big cats
   b) three sea animals
   c) holes or deep cuts in your body
   d) the place where a circus or zoo animal lives
2 Verbs that mean:
   a) train an animal to live with people
   b) hurt someone badly with nails or claws
   c) touched lightly with your fingers

DEVELOPING VOCABULARY

5 Instead of *not satisfied* and *not natural* Walter could say *dissatisfied* and *unnatural*. Add negative forms of these adjectives to a chart like the one below. Use a good dictionary to help you.

usual   practical   regular   legal   possible   logical   pleasant
kind   honest   sensitive   correct   rational   patient   moral

UN-	unnatural	DIS-	dissatisfied
IN-		IM-	
IR-		IL-	

READING

6 Read this letter from a local newspaper, and answer the questions.

1 Why has Mr Andrews written the letter?
2 In which paragraphs does he:
   a) make suggestions?   b) give opinions?

Which expressions introduce these functions?

Dear Sir/Madam

I HAVE noticed that a circus is visiting this town next week, and I am writing to express my feelings about performing animals.

Firstly, I feel that wild animals have the right to be free in their natural environments. Circuses keep animals in cages for a lot of the time, and in my opinion this is wrong. Secondly, I believe it is unnatural for any animal to be trained to do tricks. I am sure that the training involves cruelty and is therefore completely immoral.

Finally, at a time like this when people are worried about the survival of many animals, I don't think we really want to see animals humiliated, as they are in circuses.

Why don't circuses provide entertainment, such as acrobatics, which does not harm other creatures? Let's leave animals to live their lives naturally. And let's tell our local councillors that we do not want performing animals in our town.

Yours faithfully
L ANDREWS

LISTENING

7 📼 Listen to three people responding to the letter.

1 Which one has the same opinions as the writer of the letter?
2 What do the other people think about the use of animals in circuses?
3 Write three points that each speaker makes to support their opinion.

SPEECH PATTERNS

8 📼 When you disagree with someone's opinion, which part of these expressions do you stress? Practise saying them. Then listen and repeat.

*I think . . .   In my opinion . . .
As far as I'm concerned . . .*

SPEAKING

9 Discuss in groups what you think about circus animals and wild animals that are kept in zoos or as pets. Use some of the adjectives you listed in Exercise 5 and expressions from Exercise 8. Do you agree or disagree with other members of your group?

WRITING

10 Write a letter to a newspaper in response to the one on the left. Give your own opinions or give the opinion of one of your partners from Exercise 9. Start in one of these ways:

*I am writing to agree/disagree with the views that Mr Andrews expressed last week.
I sympathise with the views that Mr Andrews expressed last week, but I do not agree with everything he says.*

Language reference

GRAMMAR

1 *Be able, can* and *could*

USES

- Present tense forms of *be able* are used, like *can*, to talk about:
  natural and learned ability (skill)
  EXAMPLES: *They're all **able** to swim now. They **can** all swim now.*
  possibility
  EXAMPLES: ***Are** you **able** to come round immediately? **Can** you come round immediately?*

- *Was/were able* and *could* are used to talk about:
  past ability
  EXAMPLES: *They **were able** to perform tricks. They **could** perform tricks.*
  past possibility
  EXAMPLES: *I **was able** to go to concerts when I lived in the city. I **could** go to concerts when I lived in the city.*
  Note that the affirmative form of *could* is not usually used to refer to a single action in the past. It is, however, possible to use negative and question forms with this meaning.
  EXAMPLE: *We **couldn't** get cheap seats last night.*

- *Will be able* is used to talk about:
  future ability
  EXAMPLE: *You**'ll be able** to drive next year.*
  It is not possible to use *can* in this sense.
  future possibility
  EXAMPLE: *We**'ll be able** to go to the show next year.*
  Can is also used with this meaning.
  EXAMPLE: *We **can** go together in future.*

- *Be able* is used in structures where *can* is not possible because an infinitive form is needed.
  EXAMPLE: *He wants **to be able** to travel more.*

FORMS

- *Be able* is followed by *to* + infinitive. *Be* changes in the normal way.
  EXAMPLES: *They**'ll be able to** meet us at the box office. He **won't be able to** come.*

2 *Be able* and *manage*

- All tenses of *manage* refer to difficult achievements. The idea of 'with difficulty' is the difference between *manage* and *be able* when we use them to express possibility.
  EXAMPLE: *They **weren't able/didn't manage** to contact him.*

- *Manage* is sometimes used to express general or specific ability, also with difficulty.
  EXAMPLE: *I **manage** to type with two fingers.*

FORMS

- *Manage* is followed by *to* + infinitive. It is a regular verb and it is most commonly used in the past simple and in question forms.
  EXAMPLES: *I **managed to get** good seats. I **didn't manage to change** the other tickets. **Will** you **manage to buy** a programme before the play starts, do you think?*

FUNCTIONAL LANGUAGE

1 **Expressing ability**
   I can walk a long way.
   I'm able to walk for hours.

2 **Expressing possibility**
   He can come with us.
   He'll be able to leave work early.

3 **Talking about difficult achievements**
   Did you manage to memorise the speech?
   Will you be able to finish by tonight?

4 **Making requests**
   Can/could you help me?

5 **Talking about prohibition**
   We can't/couldn't stay out late.

6 **Giving permission**
   You can stay for an hour or two.

7 **Making deductions/guesses**
   The theatre can't be very old.
   It could be quite modern.

8 **Giving opinions**
   I feel it's wrong.
   I believe it's unnatural.
   I don't think it's right.
   In my opinion, it's unhealthy.
   As far as I'm concerned, it's immoral.

Talkback

Picture clues

Use the pictures on this page to help you play a game.

1 📼 Work in groups. Look at Pictures A–C, and listen to people playing a game. What are the rules of the game?

2 Look at Pictures D and E. Which of these words and phrases do they illustrate?
glove puppet   circus animal   modern art
amusement arcade   fashion designer
model   radio station   underground train
computer software   dress circle
pierced ears

3 Choose one of the other words or phrases in 2. Discuss how you could draw it.

4 Now play the game using the rules you heard in Exercise 1. Your teacher will give you phrases to illustrate. The first team to work out all five phrases wins.

Looking forward

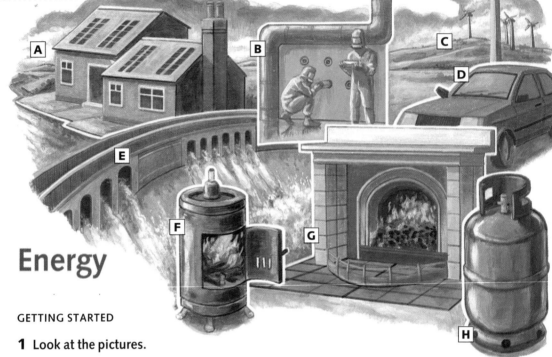

Focus

TOPICS
- Energy sources
- Life in the future

GRAMMAR
- *Will* + (adverb) + infinitive
- *Going to* + infinitive
- *May/might* + infinitive

FUNCTIONS
- Making decisions, promises, predictions
- Expressing plans and intentions
- Talking about possibilities

SKILLS
- Speaking: negotiating
- Listening: an interview, brief comments
- Writing: sentences justifying a decision
- Reading: a literary extract

Energy

GETTING STARTED

1 Look at the pictures.

1 Match them with these forms of energy:
solar power   coal   gas   wind power   nuclear energy
wood   petrol   hydroelectric power

2 Which forms are fossil fuels? Which are 'alternative' energy sources?

3 Which are renewable? Which are non-renewable?

🖭 Documentary

LISTENING

2 Before you listen, look at the pictures.

1 Where do you think this place is?
2 What form of energy is illustrated?

3 🖭 Listen to an interview with John Hoffner. Check your answers to Exercise 2 and answer these questions.

1 What is John Hoffner's job?
2 What do the two parts of the word *photovoltaics* mean?
3 How many homes can this plant provide electricity for?
4 How does John think energy use will change in the future?

4 Can you guess what these words from the interview mean?

a) predict (*v*)
b) convert (*v*)
c) plant (*n*)
d) reliance (*n*)

FOCUS ON FUNCTIONS

5 🔊 **Listen again to a short extract from the interview.**

1 Is *will* used here to:
   a) express a decision?   b) make a promise?   c) make a prediction?

2 Invent examples of affirmative and negative statements with *will* for each of the functions in 1 above.
   a) decision: *I'll take the job; it's a good one.*

3 Compare your sentences with the uses of *going to* in these examples. When do we use *going to*?
   Look at that smoke! The power station is going to explode.
   The government is going to spend a lot of money on wind power.

DISCOVERING LANGUAGE

6 🔊 **Listen to three people giving their opinions about future energy use.**

1 Which speaker:
   a) seems absolutely certain?
   b) thinks something is *probably* going to happen?
   c) thinks something will *possibly* happen, but is not sure?

2 Match these words and phrases with a–c above.
   … may/might …   … will definitely …   I think … will …

3 What kind of word follows *may/might*?

7 **Work in small groups and discuss what you think about the questions below. Use *going to, will, may* or *might*.**

1 Will fossil fuels ever run out?
2 Will nuclear power continue to be an important source of energy?
3 Will we have to change the way we live? How?

READING: A LITERARY EXTRACT

8 **Ben Elton's novel, *This Other Eden*, is set in the future. In this extract the speaker is Jurgen Thor, head of the organisation Natura.**

1 What are Jurgen's views on:
   a) people in general?   b) politicians?

2 What, in his opinion, will the consequences of man's behaviour be?

3 Do you think Rosalie agrees with his views? Do *you* agree?

'It's always been dying, ever since man began to take from it more than he needed. I tell you, Rosalie, Earth as we know it is finished, because man rules it and man is incapable of acting responsibly! Of thinking in anything other than the short-term.'
'That's just a pathetic generalisation to justify your –'
'Is it, Rosalie? Is it? Let me ask you this. What politician, facing an election next year, would be prepared to make laws, the benefit of which would not be felt until the following year! I will tell you. None. There is no *profit* to be had today in protecting tomorrow.'
Jurgen Thor had said his piece. He sat down on the floor,

br┌───┐
be│ Ben Elton is a famous British comedian and writer. He has written │
ag│ plays, novels, and TV series. │
  └───┘
various toiletries that had fallen from the bathroom cabinet. He took another great breath and leant back against the plinth of the

SPEAKING

9 **It is the year 2010. Energy resources are running low. There is no domestic gas, coal, wood or oil. A new law is announced:**

Each private home is allowed to have no more than four pieces of electrical equipment in addition to lighting. No other fuel-consuming equipment of any kind is allowed.

You live in a house with three other people and you have to decide together which four pieces of equipment to keep.

1 Work alone and write a complete list of all the household equipment that you can think of which uses electricity.

2 Discuss your lists in pairs and agree on the most important four.

3 Show your shortlist to another pair and agree on a final list.

WRITING

10 **Write sentences justifying each piece of equipment.**

We're going to keep the television …
– *because we will need information from the outside world.*
– *so that we can get information from the outside world.*

89

Focus

TOPIC
• Life in a closed ecosystem

GRAMMAR
• Articles

SKILLS
• Reading: an article
• Listening: a radio news item
• Writing: a paragraph

VOCABULARY DEVELOPMENT
• The prefix *self-*
• Compound adjectives (time and size)

Survival

GETTING STARTED

1 Look at the picture above from a newspaper article. What do you think the article is about?

READING

2 Read this article about the project in the picture. Check your answer to Exercise 1 and make brief notes under these headings:

LOCATION   SPONSOR   COST
NUMBER OF INHABITANTS
DUTIES   AIMS
CRITICISMS OF THE PROJECT

3 Work in pairs.

Student A: Without looking back at the text, use your notes to give a short talk about the project.

Student B: Listen to your partner and give help if it is needed.

Then change roles.

Bio-trekkies seek to boldly grow in glasshouse enterprise

THE TV science-fiction series *Star Trek* no longer looked far-fetched as four men and four women in black space-suits locked themselves into a giant hi-tech greenhouse, known as a 'biosphere', in the Arizona desert yesterday for a two-year study of the environment and certain ridicule by mainstream scientists.

As dawn broke over the Santa Catalina mountains, the eight waved goodbye to television cameras. Edward Bass, their multibillionaire sponsor from a Texas oil family, closed the door of the $150 million structure, with its mini-ocean, marsh, desert, savanna, rain-forest and 3,800 plant and animal species designed to allow the team to recreate Earth and its ecosystems.

The so-called Biosphere 2 is the latest of a dozen environmental projects started by the self-titled 'ecopreneur'. The project's main aim is to set up a self-sustaining community for possible use in a spaceship or on another planet. The crew members must plant, harvest and process their food on a half-acre farm in the seven-storey glass and metal structure, while conducting a series of experiments.

'We will be custodians of our new little world,' said Abigail Alling, aged 31, a US marine biologist on the team, her voice choking with emotion. 'It is a brave new step.' Many scientists, however, are more than sceptical. They point out that the largest closed ecosystem which survived more than a few days was smaller than a football. It was developed at the University of Miami and contained only shrimp, algae and other micro-organisms.

Critics have also accused Mr Bass of being more interested in producing a profitable theme park than in carrying out serious scientific research. Hundreds of tourists visited the site daily in the summer before it was occupied by the team. They paid $9.95 to enter and all stopped at the souvenir shop.

DEVELOPING VOCABULARY

4 Look back at the article.

1 In paragraph 3, which compound adjectives tell us:
   a) who gave Mr Bass the title 'ecopreneur'?
   b) who is giving help and support to the community?

2 What is the meaning of the prefix *self-*?

3 Explain the meaning of these phrases:

SELF- IN ADJECTIVES	
+ PRESENT PARTICIPLE	+ PAST PARTICIPLE
a self-locking case	a self-taught expert

SELF- IN NOUNS
classes in self-defence

4 Now make expressions with *self-* that describe:
   a) an oven that cleans itself.
   b) a woman who works for herself. (employ)
   c) a painting by an artist of his own face.

5 Check the article again.

1 Find two compound adjectives that tell us:
   a) how long the study of the environment will last. (*para. 1*)
   b) how big the farm is. (*para. 3*)

2 What are the rules for making adjectives from time periods and sizes?

3 Change these phrases to use an adjective describing the time or size:
   a guarantee for ten years
   a ten-year guarantee
   a) a wall that is two metres high
   b) a sale for ten days
   c) a house with eight storeys
   d) a lease which lasts a hundred years

DISCOVERING LANGUAGE

6 Study the text again.

1 List all the words and phrases in the text that refer to:
   a) the people in Biosphere 2.
      four men and women, …
   b) Biosphere 2.
      a giant hi-tech greenhouse, …

2 Which articles (*a/an, the*, no article) are used when the people and biosphere are:
   a) introduced for the first time?
   b) referred to later in the article?
   c) referred to by their names?

3 Can you make rules to explain the use of articles, using these phrases from the text?
   the TV science-fiction series, Star Trek;
   the Arizona desert, *the* Santa Catalina mountains
   a Texas oil family, *a* self-sustaining community, *a* US marine biologist
   mainstream scientists; shrimp, algae and other micro-organisms

7 Complete each gap with an article if one is needed.

Edward Bass is [1]..... second son of [2]..... wealthy American family, but he is not interested in [3]..... clothes, [4]..... women, or [5]..... other expensive pleasures. [6]..... millionaire takes [7]..... commercial flights and drives his own car. He used to drive [8]..... Ford Escort, but then he gave [9]..... car away and bought [10]..... Toyota. However, he loves [11]..... cowboy boots; he has a number of pairs, and he wears [12]..... boots even to very formal dinners.

LISTENING

8 You are going to hear a radio news item about Biosphere 2, broadcast two years after the article on the left appeared. Before you listen, say what you think has happened.

9 ▭ Listen to the news item. List the successes and failures of the project.

WRITING

10 Write a paragraph saying why you would or would not like to spend two years in Biosphere 2. Then show it to your partner for comment.

Discussions

1 An optimist is someone who believes that the future will be good. A pessimist thinks that it will be bad. Is the person in the cartoon an optimist or a pessimist?

Focus

TOPICS
- Genetic engineering
- Life in the future

FUNCTIONS
- Asking for explanations
- Introducing examples
- Interrupting
- Talking about certainties, probability, possibility, plans and ideas

SKILLS
- Listening: a conversation
- Speaking: discussion

SPEECH PATTERNS
- Using intonation to allow or prevent interruption

LISTENING

2 📼 Read and listen to a conversation about the future.

1 What is the specific topic that these people are discussing?
2 Which of them is a pessimist? Which is an optimist? What about the others?

ALAN: In the end science is likely to solve a lot of the world's problems ... I mean, medical advances and things like that ... *they*'ll cut down diseases. I heard a geneticist on the radio talking about how *they* might be able to get rid of hereditary diseases -5 altogether in the next ten years.

PAT: Yes ... <u>might</u>. But there are new diseases all the time. And, anyway, science creates problems ... it doesn't just solve *them*.

TIM: What do you mean? -10

PAT: Well, take genetic engineering, for instance. The same research that's intended to fight diseases has other uses as well.

ALAN: Like *what*?

PAT: Well, *they*'re not only finding out about genes that -15 cause diseases ... they're also going to know which *ones* give us the colour of our hair and eyes. In theory they already know how to create male or female children ... and now they're saying there might be a gene that affects intelligence! -20

TIM: Wait a moment. What's wrong with *that*?

PAT: What's wrong with it? Everyone'll want the same kind of children. And in some countries that'll mean mostly male children ... and all intelligent, -25 of course ... and in some countries ...

SARA: Just let me tell you something. When I have children, which I'm not thinking of doing yet, if science can give me the perfect child, then I intend to <u>have</u> the perfect child ... I think it's a great idea. -30

PAT: You see! We'll have a world full of 'perfect' people. And there'll be too many men!

ALAN: Do you really believe *that*? You can't be certain that people will choose their babies' characteristics. It would be awful if we lost the variety – I mean, if -35 people were all the same – but perhaps that won't happen. I don't think it will.

3 Which of the speakers do you think would make these comments? Which comment reflects your own views?

1 We should not interfere with genes at all.
2 It is good to be able to choose the characteristics of your child.
3 I've never thought about the problems caused by genetic engineering.
4 We can take advantage of scientific progress without worrying that research will be used in undesirable ways.

4 Look back at the conversation.

1 What do the words in *italics* refer to?
   they (line 3)
   medical advances
2 Find words or phrases that mean:
   a) reduce
   b) to stop completely
   c) passed down from one generation to the next in a family
   d) discovering
   e) has an effect on
   f) difference in quality, type or character

FOCUS ON FUNCTIONS

5 Look at the speeches in Exercise 2 again.

1 Find examples of these functions:
  a) asking for an explanation
  b) introducing an example
  c) interrupting
2 The people in this conversation know each other well. Which of these expressions for interrupting do you think are used:
  a) with people you know well?
  b) in more formal situations?
  Just a minute ...   Excuse me ...
  Could I ask a question?   Hang on ...
  Let me say something ...   Forgive me, but ...
  I'm sorry to interrupt, but ...   Listen, ...

SPEECH PATTERNS

6 🔲 Listen again to the recording of Pat's third speech.

1 Just before each pause, does her voice go up (⤴) or down (⤵)?
2 At which points in the speech is it polite to interrupt?
3 How can speakers use their voices to stop interruptions?
4 Read the extract with the same intonation patterns as Pat's.

FOCUS ON FUNCTIONS

7 Look at these verb phrases from the conversation:

A *They might/(may) ...*
B *You can't be certain ...*
C *... science is likely ...*
D *I intend ...*
E *I'm (not) thinking of ...*

1 Which phrases can be followed by:
  a) an infinitive with *to*?
  b) an infinitive without *to*?
  c) an *-ing* form?
  d) a clause with *that*?
2 Which phrase refers to:
  a) a possibility?
  b) a definite plan?
  c) a probability?
  d) a certainty?
  e) an idea that is or is not being considered?

8 John has finished university and is talking to his mother. Complete the conversation with the correct form of a suitable verb phrase.

MOTHER: So what are you going to do now?
JOHN: Well, I'm thinking of [1]..... a long holiday.
MOTHER: Yes, but I mean after that. What about work?
JOHN: Don't worry, I intend [2]..... something soon. But I want a rest first.
MOTHER: Well, don't take too long. Finding a job isn't likely [3]..... easy, you know.
JOHN: Yes, I know. I might [4]..... to people in the Careers Office. They may [5]..... to give me some ideas.
MOTHER: Yes, why don't you do that? I'm certain [6]..... some good advice.

SPEAKING

9 Work in groups of four and choose one of the topics below. Then divide into two pairs.

Pair A: You are optimists. Make notes on reasons for being optimistic about the topic.

Pair B: You are pessimists. List reasons for being pessimistic.

1 The effects of computer technology on our lives.
2 The amount of freedom that individuals will have in the future.

Discuss the topic as a group, using language from this unit if possible. Interrupt politely when you want to speak.

Language reference

GRAMMAR

1 *Going to*

USE

In this book, *going to* is used to talk about:

- plans or intentions for the future.
  EXAMPLE: *We're **going to** fly to Pisa.*
- predictions based on clear evidence.
  EXAMPLE: *Look at the sky! It's **going to** rain.*

FORMS

- Affirmative: *to be* + *going to* + infinitive (without *to*).
- Question: *to be* + subject + *going to*.
- Negative: *to be* + *not* + *going to*.

2 *Will*

In this book *will* is used to:

- express a decision made now about the future.
  EXAMPLES: *I'**ll** go by car. No, I **won't**, I'**ll** fly.*
- make predictions about the future.
  EXAMPLE: *It **will** rain tomorrow.*
- make promises.
  EXAMPLES: *I'**ll** be there on time. I **won't** be late.*

FORMS

- Affirmative: *will* (short form = *'ll*) is followed by an infinitive (without *to*).
- Question: *will* + subject.
- Negative: *will not.* (short form = *won't*)

3 Degrees of probability

Ways of expressing degrees of probability are:

- modal verbs (+ adverbs)
  Modal verbs can be used with or without particular adverbs to express:
  certainty EXAMPLE: *The Prime Minister **will** (**certainly/definitely**) call a general election.*
  probability EXAMPLE: *He **will probably** hold it in the spring.*
  possibility EXAMPLES: *He **may** postpone it until the autumn. There **could** be a new government.*
  a small possibility EXAMPLES: *There **could (perhaps)** be a new government. There **might (possibly/ perhaps)** be trouble over the results.*
- adjective + infinitive
  Some adjectives are used with an infinitive (with *to*) to express:
  certainty EXAMPLE: *Prices are **certain** to go up.*
  probability EXAMPLE: *Customers are **likely** to buy less.*

- adjective + *that* ...
  Some adjectives are used in the construction *It is* + adjective + *that* clause.
  EXAMPLE: *It is **certain/likely/ probable/possible** that they will be late home.*
  If a past tense form of *to be* is used after *it*, tense changes in the *that* clause follow the rules for reported speech.
  EXAMPLE: *It **was likely** that they **would be** late home.*

4 Articles

Some useful general rules for the use of articles are:

- We use an indefinite article, *a/an*, to introduce new information or to refer to one of a class of things.
  EXAMPLES: *She saw **a** man. He ... I need **a** new pen.*
- We use the definite article, *the*, to refer to information that we share with our listeners/readers, to identify a particular thing or when there is only one of something.
  EXAMPLES: *It was an experiment, and in many ways **the** experiment was successful. **The** Arizona desert.*
- We do not use an article with plural or uncountable nouns when we are talking generally about things.
  EXAMPLES: ***Scientists** believe there will be problems. **Petrol** has become much more expensive.*

FUNCTIONAL LANGUAGE

1 Expressing a decision
I won't go now. I'll go later.

2 Making a promise
I'll ring you next week, I promise.

3 Making a prediction
We will run out of oil in the next fifty years.
I've seen the figures and oil is going to run out.

4 Talking about probability
Peter will (definitely) be here by ten o'clock.
Jane will probably come later.
She's likely to come by taxi.
There may/could/might be a delay.

5 Interrupting someone
Just a minute. Can I say something?

6 Talking about intentions
They're going to check the accounts.
They intend to investigate the problems.

7 Introducing an example
Take genetic engineering, for instance.

8 Asking for an explanation
What do you mean?

GRAMMAR AND FUNCTIONS

1 Complete each gap in the news report with an appropriate form of *can*, *could*, *be able* or *manage*.

The Mississippi River broke its banks last night and caused flooding over a very wide area. Police helicopters flew over the area this morning to assess the damage. 'When darkness lifted, we ¹..... to identify people who were on the roofs of their houses. The rescue services ²..... rescue all of them this morning, but I am sure they ³..... to reach them before it gets dark again.'

We spoke to some of the people rescued from their homes. 'Everyone in my family ⁴..... swim, but the water was rising too fast. I was worried about my elderly mother, but fortunately she ⁵..... to get onto the roof.'

People here ⁶..... understand what has gone wrong. 'There are strong river defences and we understood that we ⁷..... live here safely. I don't think we ⁸..... to stay here now. It's much too dangerous.'

2 Write sentences with a similar meaning to the ones below. Use the words in brackets.

1 We'll move next year.
   a) (definitely)   b) (certain)
2 The company will probably leave London.
   a) (likely)   b) (probable)
3 Perhaps it will move to Manchester.
   a) (may)   b) (possible)

3 Match each question with the best answer.

1 Is that Richard Gere?
2 Could he act in those days?
3 Could I see the programme?
4 Can I say something?
5 What did you think of the film?

A As far as I'm concerned, it was a waste of money.
B Most people thought so.
C No, it can't be.
D Yes, here you are.
E Yes. What is it?

4 Tony has planned a party. Complete his friend's questions about his plans (using *going to*) and about decisions that he needs to make (using *will*).

1 *When .....?   Next Saturday.*
   What time ..... start?
2 *Where .....?   In the garden.*
   ..... big enough?
3 *How many .....?   Thirty or forty.*
   ..... your parents?
4 *How much food .....?   Very little.*
   ..... home-made?
5 *..... a band?   No, I'm not.*
   ..... your stereo outside?

5 Correct any mistakes in the use of articles in this paragraph.

> Tony had his party and party was a great success. There wasn't the band, but there was music and a people danced to it. Tony's neighbours came too, so the party did not move into a house until after midnight. The Tony's friends were still enjoying themselves at three in morning.

VOCABULARY

6 Change the phrases below into shorter noun phrases (adjective + noun).

an act that is not legal   *an illegal act*

   1 people who are not responsible
   2 an organisation that governs itself
   3 an experience that is not pleasant
   4 a race that is ten miles long
   5 parents who sacrifice themselves
   6 an answer that is not correct
   7 people who have educated themselves
   8 a note with a value of ten pounds
   9 a solution that is not practical
  10 a customer who is not satisfied

Making news

Focus

TOPIC
• Newspapers

GRAMMAR
• Past simple passive

SKILLS
• Listening: a monologue
• Reading: newspaper extracts

GETTING STARTED

1 Look at these jobs in the newspaper business. Which two words mean the same?

journalist   editor   deputy editor
reporter   cartoonist   critic
foreign correspondent   sub-editor

Match the people with their responsibilities.

1 opinions on plays and books
2 reports from abroad
3 the content of the newspaper; comments on stories and issues
4 news stories
5 corrections to articles and design
6 comic drawings with captions
7 the newspaper, when the boss is away

🎧 Documentary

LISTENING

2 Before you listen, discuss these questions in pairs.

1 The *Guinness Book of Records* says that the world's heaviest newspaper was an edition of the Sunday *New York Times*. Do you think it weighed more than:
a) 2 kilos?   b) 4 kilos?   c) 6 kilos?

2 What is the biggest newspaper in your country? How many different sections has it got? What are they?

3 🎧 Ivan Fallon works for a newspaper called *The Sunday Times*, which is published in London. Listen to an interview with him and answer these questions.

1 How many sections are there in *The Sunday Times*?
2 Which sections does he refer to?

4 🎧 Listen again and answer these questions.

1 Which is bigger: a broadsheet newspaper or a tabloid?
2 What is the 'leader' and who writes it?
3 Which section does Ivan Fallon edit?
4 What is special about the book section?

READING

5 *The Sunday Times* changed just after the interview. Look at the picture below.

1 How many sections are there now?
2 What is the name of the general arts section that Ivan Fallon referred to?
3 Which of the sections that he mentioned has disappeared?
4 Which section would you read first? Why?

[1] OH BOY! A TRAMPOLINE!

[2] Top savings rates

Compound annual interest (CAR), %

BIGGEST SOCIETIES	Notice	Gross	Net of tax at 25%
Bristol & West	Instant		
Birmingham Midshires			
Woolwich			

[3] # TURKEY

Your unique, made to measure experience. Discreet hotels, mansions, Sultans' Palaces, exclusive farmhouses, villas with pools and mini-cruises – you choose – we tailor a holiday or tour just for you. Pampered luxury, exceptional

THE first convoy of evacuees from Sarajevo in nearly a year was cancelled yesterday after tensions between Croat and Muslim forces, which have exploded elsewhere in the country, reached breaking point in the Bosnian capital.

[4] ONE of the most charismatic figures of the former Soviet army, General Boris Gromov – long regarded as the communist officer corps' most likely Bonaparte – is believed by fellow officers to be at last making his bid for supreme leadership of Russia's armed forces.

HOPES of an advance in the peace talks in Northern Ireland were raised yesterday when Albert Reynolds, the Irish Prime Minister, signalled that Dublin was prepared to amend its territorial claim to the province.

[5] ## Just Tell Me When To Cry

by Richard Fleischer

Souvenir £16.99 pp350

When, midway through writing his third volume of autobiography, the 'I' broke off Peter Bull's typewriter, he took it as a sign and immediately started a chapter about the other people in his life.

© D.C. Thomson & Co, Ltd 1994 / 'The Dandy'

[6] ### ARIES (March 20 – April 19)

If you intend to bring order to the practical side of your life, and particularly to deal with financial or investment matters, then the next few weeks are just what you need.

[8] ### Boxing

Phil Martin, the manager of Tony Ekubia, has issued a High Court writ against the British Boxing Board of Control for blocking Ekubia's challenge for the European light-welter-weight title against Christian Merle, the

[7] IAIN JOHNSTONE on
Jane Campion's The Piano

It must be the aim of every sensitive and sentient film director to make a movie that will attract acclaim as a work of art and attract an audience. The two are often mutually exclusive, but Jane Campion may have come close with The Piano.

[9] ## SUGAR INDUSTRY

A cane sugar refinery in a developing country in the Caribbean wishes to recruit an experienced expert in:
Purchasing raw sugar
Managing refining operations

[10] VIOLENT crime is up by 40% over five years, one-third of births are illegitimate, and in many towns and cities a benefit culture is suppressing any possibility of the emergence of an enterprise culture. Few any longer deny that an underclass is being created in Britain. But the government has yet to recognise the problem, let alone act on it.

---

6 Look at the extracts above from *The Sunday Times*. Find the extracts that are:

a) about money
b) a film review
c) a travel advertisement
d) a job advertisement
e) news reports
f) a book review
g) comments on life in Britain
h) for children
i) from horoscopes
j) about sport

7 Which section of the paper do you think each extract comes from?

8 Look at this example of the present passive from news extracts 4 above.

General Boris Gromov ... is believed by fellow officers to be ...

1 How do you think we make *past* passive verb forms?
2 Find two examples of past passives in the news extracts.
3 Why do you think the writers have used passive and not active forms of the verbs?

9 Change these headlines about yesterday's news into sentences that include past passive forms.

Vicious dog attacks child in park

A child was attacked by a vicious dog in a park yesterday.

1 Storm hits South of England
2 Bosses lock factory gates
3 Council sacks head teacher
4 Chancellor announces new taxes
5 Tottenham beat Liverpool
6 Police arrest 8-year-old boy

10 Look at the picture and describe what was done to the child in the school playground.

Child gangs terrorise schools

97

Focus

TOPICS
- Objectivity and bias in newspapers
- Reading habits

GRAMMAR
- Present perfect passive

SKILLS
- Reading: comments for a survey
- Listening: short interviews
- Speaking: discussion, an interview
- Writing: a report

SPEECH PATTERNS
- Word stress

Reading habits

🔄 COMPARING CULTURES

1 Which are the most important newspapers in your country? Describe them, using these guidelines to help you:

- frequency: *daily/weekly paper*
- size: *broadsheet/tabloid*
- photographs: *colour/black and white*
- political views: *left-wing/right-wing/politically neutral*
- ownership: *government-owned/owned by a political party/independent*
- language: *serious/sensational; difficult/simple*

When you read a newspaper, which do you read, and why?

READING

2 Read this quote about British newspapers. Then complete the chart below to show the woman's preferences.

❝ I don't often read newspapers during the week – I haven't got time. I take a Sunday paper, though. I like serious newspapers because I know the articles have been written by journalists who are well informed. I hate all those sensational stories in the tabloids. They're so biased and they're full of half-truths – I can't believe they're allowed to publish some of them. And I can't stand the chequebook journalism that goes on. You know that some criminal has been paid thousands of pounds to tell their awful story. It makes me sick. ❞

TYPE OF NEWSPAPER	FREQUENCY	REASONS FOR CHOOSING THIS NEWSPAPER	REASONS FOR NOT CHOOSING OTHERS

3 Choose the best meaning for these words and phrases:

1 sensational
   a) boring   b) shocking
   c) honest

2 biased
   a presentation of the facts that is:
   a) fair   b) unfair
   c) completely dishonest

3 a half-truth
   a statement that is:
   a) false   b) true
   c) true but not complete

4 chequebook journalism
   journalism which:
   a) pays journalists well
   b) pays well for all interviews
   c) pays well for shocking stories

LISTENING

4 🔊 Listen to three other people being interviewed about daily papers and, where possible, add information about their preferences to your chart from Exercise 2.

5 🔊 Listen again and answer these questions.

1 What does the first man mean by 'objective'?
2 What does the woman mean by 'human interest' stories?
3 Who does the second man mean by 'the royals'? Give some examples of other 'public figures'.

SPEECH PATTERNS

6 🔊 Look at these words and say them to yourself:

sensation   education   information
imagination   edition   production

1 Mark the main stress on each word. Then listen and check.
2 What general rule can you make about the pronunciation of words ending in *-tion*? Can you think of other words with the same ending?
3 Now listen again and repeat the words.

DISCOVERING LANGUAGE

7 Look at these examples of the present perfect passive:

A *The articles **have been written** by journalists who are well informed.*
B *... some criminal **has been paid** thousands of pounds ...*
C *They***'ve been taken** *over by companies who have political interests.*

1 How is the present passive formed?
2 Why do speakers use the passive rather than the active verb form in the examples?
3 What *time* is referred to in each of the examples?
4 Make rules that explain when it is appropriate to use the present perfect passive.

8 Complete the gaps in this radio report using past passive or present perfect passive verb forms.

Storms in south-east England caused severe damage to property last night. On the south coast, the sea burst through sea walls and hundreds of houses ¹..... (flood). Between midnight and 4 a.m. cars ²..... (overturn) and trees ³..... (tear) from the ground. Two people ⁴..... (kill) when their car ⁵..... (blow) off the M25 motorway into a ditch. Thousands of people ⁶..... injured.

The storm seems to be over now, and casualties ⁷..... (take) to emergency centres all over the region. People whose homes ⁸..... (damage) ⁹..... (give) accommodation in hotels and guesthouses.

SPEAKING

9 Work in pairs. Discuss the kinds of newspaper and magazine features that are popular in your country. Consider the topics below, and mention examples of articles that you have read recently.

human interest stories   animals   sport
public figures   foreign news   disasters
the environment   health and beauty   fashion
reviews   national politics

10 Interview your partner about his/her reading habits and make notes. Ask about newspapers, magazines and comics. Use these question words:

What ...?   Which ...?   How often ...?
Why ...?   When ...?   Where ...?

WRITING

11 Now write about your partner's reading habits. Here is an example:

Soraya does not read a newspaper every day but she buys one occasionally to read on the bus. She usually chooses a serious paper because she likes reading reviews of new films and plays. However, she sometimes buys a tabloid if she's attracted by the headline on the front page and if she wants to read the news quickly. She never buys comics, but she sometimes looks at her brother's Batman comics. The only magazine she buys is about computer games, and that is because there is usually a free computer disk.

Changing perspectives

Focus

TOPIC
• Perspectives on events

SKILLS
• Speaking: interpreting events
• Reading: a narrative
• Writing: a perspective on events; a newspaper report

VOCABULARY DEVELOPMENT
• Adjectives and their connotations

GETTING STARTED

1 Look at two headlines that appeared in different newspapers on the same day. Answer the questions below.

> **A** SYDNEY WINS RIGHT TO STAGE OLYMPIAD 2000

> **B** Olympics misery as Brits' bid fails

1 Which two countries are referred to in the headlines?
2 What were they competing for?
3 Which country won the competition?
4 Which headline reports:
   a) a reaction?   b) a fact?
5 Which headline is from:
   a) a serious newspaper?   b) a tabloid?
6 How do you think people in Sydney felt? Change words in the second headline to report the event from their point of view.

SPEAKING

2 Study the picture carefully. Work with your partner.

1 Where are the people?
2 What time of day is it?
3 What has just happened?
4 What do you think is going to happen next?

3 We can interpret the picture in a number of ways. Here are two possible scenarios. Can you think of any others?

1 The younger man is going to attack the elderly couple.
2 The younger man has stopped to help the elderly couple.

DEVELOPING VOCABULARY

4 If your interpretation matches Scenario 1 above, you see the elderly couple as victims and the younger man as an attacker. Read this account by someone who watched them through binoculars from a distant house.

1 List words and phrases that the writer uses to build a frightening picture of the younger man.
2 List words and phrases that the writer uses to describe the couple as helpless victims.

It is a very dark, isolated road. An elderly couple broke down and did not seem to know what to do. A car pulled up behind them and then the lights were turned off.

I saw a huge, ugly-looking man of about thirty get out of the car. He looked terrifying. He had long, greasy hair which hung over the collar of his leather jacket, and he was wearing filthy, torn jeans and big, black, leather boots. He was holding a large metal tool in his hand, which he waved in the air as he walked slowly towards the couple's car. The old man lifted his arm weakly to greet him, and then took a couple of unsteady steps backwards. His wife looked nervously at the young man and then at her husband. The old people both seemed so vulnerable.

5 The adjectives below can describe a frightening person or a helpless person.

powerful   muscular   powerless   defenceless
angry   frightened   worried   frightening
sinister   harmless   evil   innocent   strong
feeble   naive   weak   loud   gentle   silent
sharp   terrified   confused   trusting
aggressive   frail   threatening

1 Divide them into the two groups.
2 Find some words that have:
   a) similar meanings.   b) opposite meanings.
3 Which of these words can be used, as adjectives or adverbs, to refer to:
   a) physical features?   *He had powerful arms ...*
   b) feelings?   *She was angry ...*
   c) character?   *He was a naive man ...*
   d) ways of speaking?   *She spoke sharply ...*
   e) ways of moving?   *He walked aggressively ...*
4 List adjectives that can be used to describe:
   a) a helpful person.
   b) a person who is not afraid.

WRITING

6 Work in pairs. Using some of the words above to help you, write a description of exactly the same moments that are described in Exercise 4, but from one of the following perspectives.

1 You are the younger man. You have stopped your car to help the couple.
2 You are the younger man. You intend to rob them.
3 You are the old man or the old woman. You believe that the younger man is going to rob you.
4 You are the old man or the old woman. You believe that the younger man has stopped to help you.

7 Try to improve what you have written. Have you conveyed the atmosphere of the incident? Do you need to add any sentences to give more suspense? Can you improve the vocabulary you have used?

8 Write a short newspaper report about the incident, in which the couple were, in fact, robbed.

Language reference

1 The past simple passive

USES

We use past passive forms:

- when we do not know who performed an action.
  EXAMPLE: *Money and keys **were taken** from coat pockets during the party.*
- when information about who performed the action is uninteresting, unimportant or obvious. The past simple passive is common in certain kinds of reports, such as reports of:
  crimes and legal procedures
  EXAMPLE: *A woman **was sentenced** to two years in prison.*
  accidents and natural disasters
  EXAMPLES: *A child **was hurt**. Buildings **were damaged**.*
  academic research
  EXAMPLE: *Three millilitres of water **were added** to the mixture.*
- to focus on the action and the person/thing affected by the action. Compare the emphasis in these sentences:
  active
  *A bus completely **destroyed** my car yesterday.*
  passive
  *My car was completely **destroyed** yesterday.*
- to avoid beginning a sentence with a complex subject.
  EXAMPLE: *Most fish **are caught** by **fishermen who are prepared to wait patiently on the river bank in all weathers.***

The past simple passive is used rather than the present perfect passive when events happened at a specific time in the past.

FORMS

- The past simple passive is formed with *was/were* + a past participle.
  EXAMPLES: *She **was arrested**. They **were** both **taken** away.*
- We use *by* to say who performed the action.
  EXAMPLE: *The fruit was picked **by** students.*

2 The present perfect passive

USES

Like other passive forms, the present perfect passive is used:

- when the performer of an action is unknown, uninteresting, unimportant or obvious.
  EXAMPLE: *The President **has been shot**!*
- to focus on the action and the person/thing affected by the action.
  EXAMPLE: ***My car** has been scratched!*
- to avoid beginning a sentence with a complex subject.
  EXAMPLE: *He's just **been attacked** by **the man his girlfriend used to go out with***.

The present perfect passive is used rather than the past passive to refer to:

- events that happened at an unspecified time in the recent or distant past.
  EXAMPLE: *The match **has been cancelled**.*
- a situation that began at a point in the past and continues to the present moment.
  EXAMPLE: *They **have been neglected** for years/since they were small children.*

FORMS

- The present perfect passive is formed with *have/has been* + a past participle.
  EXAMPLE: *She **has been given** a new hotel room.*
- We use *by* to say who performed the action.
  EXAMPLE: *This article has been checked **by** a sub-editor.*

Talkback

A critical eye

The pictures below illustrate the development of television.

1 Discuss these questions in pairs:
When was television invented? When did it become popular in your country? What did people watch and listen to before television was available?

How has television changed since its invention? What features of television do you like and dislike?

How is television likely to change in the future? What improvements would you like to see?

2 Continue working with your partner. Discuss the questions from 1 in relation to the objects shown in the photographs. Note down your views.

3 Find a new partner and compare notes. Do you agree with each other?

4 Report back to your original partner. What do you think now? Are there changes that you would like to make to your original notes?

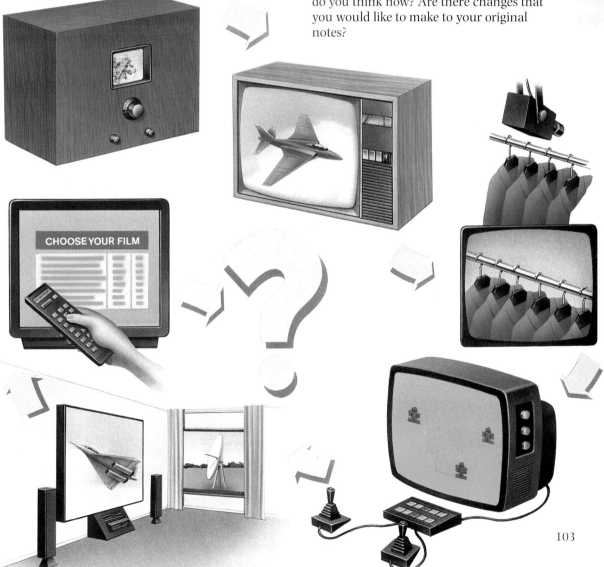

13 | *On show*

But is it art?

Focus

TOPICS
- Exhibitions
- Art

GRAMMAR
- Past perfect simple

SKILLS
- Reading: an article
- Writing: describing an experience

VOCABULARY DEVELOPMENT
- *Go* + adjective

Jelly sculpture goes out with the leftovers

ART STUDENT Ceri Davies had spent months planning her exhibit – 34 red jellies displayed on 17 plates set out in an arc on the floor of the Midlands Arts Centre, Birmingham.

The work was meant to be on display for three weeks and Ms Davies' intention was that as time passed the jewel-like jellies would begin to gather mould and decay, offering a visual metaphor for the way the human body decays after death. On the fourth day of the exhibition, however, a member of staff mistook her creation for the leftovers from a party at the centre's restaurant and, scraping the jellies from their plates, dumped them in a nearby dustbin.

'I couldn't believe my eyes. Months of hard work had just gone to waste. I was quite horrified,' said Ms Davies, who is taking a Master of Arts course at the University of Central England, Birmingham. 'The actual jellies didn't take long to make, but months of thought and planning had gone into their creation. When I first made them, they looked jewel-like, very fresh, shiny and red. The whole point of the exhibition was that the jellies should shrivel, change shape and go dull and mouldy. I wanted to use food that resembled the body in some way and to remind people of what happens after they die. The jellies had just started to go mouldy when the officer in charge of the building for some reason just collected up the plates and scraped the jelly off.'

A spokeswoman for the centre said, 'It was a genuine mistake and the person is very sorry. But one of the jellies was really mouldy and smelling badly. They hadn't put a sign to suggest it was part of an exhibition.'

GETTING STARTED

1 Work in pairs and discuss these questions.

1 Have you ever seen any really famous works of art? What were they? Where did you see them? What did you think of them?
2 Look at the pictures. Do you think that jellies on plates are 'art'?
3 What would you add to or change in this definition of art?
   Art is the making or expression of what is beautiful.

READING

2 Before you read the article, look at the pictures again, and read the headline.

1 Why do you think the woman looks so miserable?
2 List vocabulary that a writer could use to refer to:
   a) a jelly sculpture   b) an art exhibition

3 Read the article and check your answers to Exercise 2.

4 Now answer questions about the article.

1 What exactly was Ceri's exhibit?
2 For how many days was it on show?
3 Who removed her exhibit, and why?
4 What did the sculpture represent?
5 Which words and phrases are used to describe the jellies:
   a) at the start of the exhibition?
   b) after a few days?

Guess the meaning of new words and then check with a dictionary.

DEVELOPING VOCABULARY

5 Over time, the jellies *went mouldy*. Use *go* + one of the adjectives below to answer the questions, describing a change of state.

bald   red   bad   blind   grey

What happens to:
1 your hair as you get older? *It ...*
2 meat after a few days? *It ...*
3 you as you lose your hair? *You ...*
4 your face when you are embarrassed? *It ...*
5 you if you lose your sight? *You ...*

DISCOVERING LANGUAGE

6 Look at these examples of the past perfect in sentences from the article:

A *The actual jellies didn't take long to make, but months of thought and planning **had gone** into their creation.*
B *They **hadn't put** a sign to suggest it was part of an exhibition.*

1 How is the past perfect simple formed? Make a rule.
2 Which of the two events in Sentence A happened first?
   a) Ceri made the jellies.
   b) She thought about the sculpture and planned it.
   What does the past perfect tell us about the time sequence?
3 Look at Sentence B. Was a sign necessary *before* or *after* the jellies were thrown away?

7 Answer these questions about Ceri's situation. Use a past perfect verb form in your answer.

1 Why was Ceri unhappy on the fourth day of the exhibition? (someone/throw away/jellies)
2 What had she done before she made the jellies? (she/plan/sculpture)
3 How had she displayed them in the museum?
4 What had the museum official done?
5 Why hadn't he thought that the jellies were an exhibit?

WRITING

8 Think about a time when you were very unhappy or disappointed. Then work in pairs and interview your partner. Ask when this was, what had happened to make them unhappy, and what they did to make themselves feel better again. Write about your partner's experience.

A

B

C

Focus

TOPIC
• Museums

FUNCTIONS
• Asking for and giving directions

SKILLS
• Reading: an extract from a brochure
• Listening: two short talks
• Speaking: a short talk, a role play

Learning experiences

GETTING STARTED

1 Look at the pictures.

1 Which picture shows a museum of:
   a) chocolate making?
   b) science and technology?
   c) an international organisation?

2 What do you think you can see in each of the museums?

2 Think about the last museum you went to.

1 What was it called? What did it specialise in?

2 Was there anything you could do apart from look at the exhibits?

3 What did you like/dislike about it?

4 What other specialist museums have you heard about?

Documentary

LISTENING

3 🔲 **Listen to Alison Porter, a museum curator, talking about a gallery at one of the museums in the pictures.**

1 Which museum is she talking about?

2 Why was this gallery special when it opened?

3 How many different exhibits are there?

4 Who usually visits the gallery:
   a) on weekdays?   b) at the weekends?

5 Alison Porter gives two reasons why she thinks visitors find the gallery stimulating. What are they?

READING

4 Before you read, look again at Picture B.

1 Do you know the name of this organisation? What is its main work? When do you think it was started?

2 Why do you think the organisation has two symbols?

5 Read the text and check your answers to Exercise 4.

The International Red Cross and Red Crescent Museum was opened in Geneva in 1988. It tells the story of men and women who, in the course of the major events of the last 150 years, have given assistance to victims of wars and natural disasters.

The organisation was established in 1863, and was based on an idea by a Swiss businessman called Henry Dunant. He had witnessed the appalling casualties at the Battle of Solferino in Italy four years earlier, in which 40,000 people were killed, wounded or missing. He had seen the lack of medical services and the great suffering of many of the wounded, who simply died from lack of care. The International Red Cross/Red Crescent exists to help the victims of conflicts and disasters regardless of their nationality.

The symbol of the organisation was originally just the red cross. It has no religious significance; the founders of the movement adopted it as a tribute to Switzerland. However, during the Russo-Turkish War (1875–8), Turks felt that the cross could be seen as offensive to Muslim soldiers and a second symbol, the red crescent, was adopted for use by national organisations in the Islamic world. Both are now official symbols.

6 Think about these questions.

1 When was the Battle of Solferino?
2 In what way is the red cross symbol 'a tribute to Switzerland'?
3 Why was the red cross seen as possibly offensive to Muslim soldiers?
4 What would you expect to see on a visit to the museum? Is there anything you would now like to add to your ideas in Exercise 1?

LISTENING

7 🎞 Listen to a guide talking about what the museum contains.

1 Which of these exhibits of the museum does she mention?
   a) the Wall of Time
   b) copies of the original Red Cross agreements
   c) an exhibition of war poetry
   d) examples of early medical kits
   e) an index of First World War prisoners
   f) a room describing work against AIDS
   g) films of wartime and peacetime activities
   h) TV programmes on present-day activities
2 Does she mention any other special features?

8 🎞 All the words below are taken from the guide's talk. Put the words into pairs which have a similar meaning in the talk. Then listen again and see if you were right.

exhibit   fascinating   card index system   records   wars
conflicts   work   casualties   activities   interesting   victims
misery   suffering   display

SPEAKING

9 Work in pairs.
Student A: Talk in detail about a museum you have been to. Describe what you can see there. Use these phrases to help you:
There are …   It's got …
You can see …   One room has …
X is shown/displayed …
Another interesting feature is …
It leaves you feeling …
Student B: Give help if your partner needs it. Ask questions at the end for more information.

FOCUS ON FUNCTIONS

10 Name places in a museum where you can:

a) get a drink
b) leave your coat
c) buy postcards
d) wash your hands
e) leave the building
f) buy tickets
g) buy a meal
h) eat your own food
i) buy a book
j) use reference books

11 Work in pairs.

1 **Student B:** You work for a museum. Turn to page 128 and answer your partner's questions.
   Student A: You are a visitor to a British museum. Ask for directions to places a) – e) above. Use these expressions to help you, and make notes on where the places are.

   Excuse me, | is there a/an …?
                | I'm looking for …
                | which floor is … on?
                | how do I get to …?

2 Change roles.
   Student A: Turn to page 128 and answer your partner's questions.
   Student B: Ask for directions to places f) – j) and make notes.

3 Check your notes against the museum plan on page 128.

Childhood

I used to think that grown-up people chose
To have stiff backs and wrinkles round their
   nose,
And veins like small fat snakes on either
   hand,
On purpose to be grand.
Till through the banisters I watched one day
My great-aunt Etty's friend, who was going
   away,
And how her onyx beads had come
   unstrung.
I saw her grope to find them as they rolled;
And then I saw that she was helplessly old,
As I was helplessly young.

> This poem is taken from *Collected Poems* by Frances Cornford, a British poet who lived from 1886 to 1960.

Responding to pictures

READING: A POEM

1 Read the poem above. What characteristic does the poet think children and old people share?

2 Match these words to the explanations below.

grown-up   wrinkles   veins   grand
banisters   beads

a) small balls worn on a string around your neck
b) tubes that carry blood around the body
c) rails at the side of stairs to hold on to
d) adult
e) attractive and formal
f) lines in older people's skin

3 Now answer these questions about the poem.

1 What qualities did the girl use to think adults had?
2 Does she describe the features of old people in a positive or a negative way in the first four lines?
3 Describe the event that changed her mind.
4 Do you agree with her conclusion? Can you give other examples of this similarity between elderly people and children?

SPEAKING

4 Work in groups of four. Choose one of the topics below for discussion. Note down the main points that are made by people in the group, and then summarise the group's views to the class.

a) Children with rich parents are likely to be happier than children with poor parents.
b) Children should not have adult rights or responsibilities until they are eighteen.

5 The photographs above are part of a series from a magazine.

1 What do you think the subject of the series of photographs is?
2 Which picture do you like best? Why?

FOCUS ON FUNCTIONS

6 📼 **Listen to a woman describing one of the photographs.**

1 Which picture is she describing?
2 Match the expressions that the speaker uses with their purpose:

a) *in the middle ... behind ...*   describing people
b) *they're wearing ... they've got ...*   (what you can see)
c) *they look ... they (don't) seem ...*   expressing your feelings
d) *I think ... in my opinion ...*   describing location
e) *it makes me feel ...*   describing people
      (what you can guess)
      expressing opinions

7 📼 **Listen again. Note the words and phrases that the speaker uses when she hesitates. Which expressions in your language have a similar function?**

DEVELOPING VOCABULARY

8 Find pairs of adjectives in this list with similar or opposite meanings. Not all the words form pairs. How many can you find?

lonely   rich   hungry
helpless   weak   healthy
neglected   ill   spoilt
innocent   cheerful   carefree
well-fed   miserable   arrogant
vulnerable   elegant   wealthy
proud   relaxed   lively
anxious   hopeful

9 Work in pairs. Choose three adjectives from the list that you could use to describe each child. Then discuss your choices with other students.

SPEAKING

10 Work in pairs.

Student A: Choose a different picture and describe:
a) what you can see.
b) what you can guess about the person/situation.
c) what the picture makes you feel.

Student B: Ask your partner questions for more information.

Then change roles.

Language reference

The past perfect simple

USE

- The past perfect simple is used to refer to events that happened *before* other events in the past. We use it to be clear about this time relationship. EXAMPLES: *When I got there, she* **had left**. *She* **had learnt** *to read and write by her fifth birthday.*

FORMS

- The past perfect simple is formed with *had* + a past participle.
  Affirmative   *She* **had left***.*
  Negative   *She* **had not (hadn't) left***.*
  Question   ***Had** she* **left***?*
  Short answers   *Yes, she* **had***./No, she* **hadn't***.*

CONJUNCTIONS

Certain conjunctions are common in sentences that contain past perfect clauses, for example, *when, before, by the time, after, as soon as.*
Note these constructions:

- (past perfect clause) | ***when*** / ***before*** / ***by the time*** | (past simple clause)

  EXAMPLE: *The dancing* **had begun before** *we* **arrived***.*

- ***After*** / ***As soon as*** / ***When*** | (past perfect clause), (past simple clause)

  EXAMPLE: ***As soon as** the dancing* **had finished***, they* **left** *the room.*

ADVERBS

Certain adverbs are also common with past perfect verb forms, for example, *just, already, yet, ever, never, before.*

- We put *just, already, ever* and *never* between *had* and the past participle. EXAMPLES: *I* **had just turned** *the corner when the accident happened. He was the nicest man I* **had ever met***.*
- *Before* in this use always comes at the end of the clause. EXAMPLE: *We* **hadn't been** *there* **before***.*
- *Yet* can come at the end of the clause or, in a negative statement, between *hadn't* and the past participle. EXAMPLES: ***Had** he* **made** *the beds* **yet***? He* **hadn't yet made** *the beds.*

FUNCTIONAL LANGUAGE

1 Describing what there is
There are sixty exhibits.
The museum has (got) a coffee shop.
You can see some lovely sculptures.
Another interesting feature is the interactive gallery.

2 Asking for directions
Excuse me. Is there a bookshop?
I'm looking for the toilets.
Which floor is the café on?
How do I get to the lift?
What's the best way of getting to the Rodin exhibition?

3 Giving directions
It's upstairs/downstairs/on the first floor/near the entrance.
Go up the escalator to the second floor.
Take the lift to the top floor.

4 Describing location
He's in the middle of a garden in front of a palace.

5 Describing people
They're wearing nappies.
He's got short dark hair.
They look unhappy.
He doesn't seem very relaxed.

6 Giving opinions
I think their parents are quite wealthy.
In my opinion, this situation is absolutely shocking.

7 Describing reactions
It leaves you feeling sad.
It makes me feel happy.

8 Hesitating
. . . er . . . em . . .
. . . let me see, . . .
. . . you know . . .

Progress check Units 12–13

GRAMMAR AND FUNCTIONS

1 Read part of the schedule of a group of British tourists in China, and then look at how they spent their free day. Write dialogues, like the example, about these people:

1 Jane and Tom   2 Lenny and Pam   3 Tricia

What did David do on the last day?
He explored the Forbidden City.
Had he explored it before?
Yes, he had.

BEIJING

Day 1	a.m.	Great Wall	p.m.	Ming Tombs
Day 2	a.m.	the Forbidden City	p.m.	Lama Temple
Day 3	all day	free time		

GUANZHOU

Free day

David: explore the Forbidden City
Jane and Tom: shop at the Friendship Store
Lenny and Pam: walk on the Great Wall
Tricia: visit the Summer Palace

2 Look again at the schedule. Complete the sentences with an adverb or conjunction.

when   by the time   just   already   yet   never

1 On the first day, they drove to the Ming Tombs ..... they had had lunch.
2 When they had lunch on that first day, they had ..... seen the Great Wall.
3 Before the last day, Jane and Tom had ..... been to the Friendship Store.
4 David spent his free day at the Forbidden City, but he had ..... been there.
5 Tricia chose to go to the Summer Palace because she had not visited it ......
6 The group had spent three days in Beijing ..... they left for Guanzhou.

3 Change these active sentences into passive ones. Use the original subject if you think it is important.

1 Benfica beat Manchester United last night.
2 The crowd invaded the pitch after the match.
3 Outside the ground they smashed shop windows.
4 Police have arrested over a hundred people.
5 Doctors have treated more than fifty people for minor injuries.

4 Look at the picture. Complete the questions and answers.

1 What's the best way ..... getting to the office?
..... the bus. It stops outside.
2 Which floor is Transworld .....?
The ..... floor.
3 Is ..... a lift?
No, we have to ..... the stairs, I'm afraid.
4 ..... do I get to the stairs?
They're ..... the entrance. But don't worry, I'll come and meet you ..... at the reception desk.

VOCABULARY

5 Answer the questions using a form of *go* + one of the adjectives below.

crazy   deaf   black   cold   wrong

1 Is there any more soup? *Yes, but .....*
2 Why didn't he hear me? *He .....*
3 Why are you so upset? *Everything ..... today.*
4 What happened when you told her about the theft? *She .....*
5 Is your finger hurting? *Yes, the nail .....*

Door to door

Focus

TOPIC
• Couriers

GRAMMAR
• Reported speech

SKILLS
• Reading: an article, an advertisement
• Listening: a conversation
• Speaking: reporting an experience

GETTING STARTED

1 **List all the ways in which you can send an urgent message or parcel to someone in your own country and abroad. Which methods are quickest/ slowest? Which are most/ least expensive?**

READING

2 **Before you read, look at the headline and introduction to the article.**

1 How is it possible to travel from Britain to Brazil and back for £200?

2 Match words from each list to make phrases that you might find in the article. What does each phrase mean?
express delivery = a very fast mail delivery service

LIST A
express   customs   hand
fare-paying   return
full-fare   last-minute

LIST B
ticket   luggage   flight
bargain   delivery
passenger   procedures

3 **Look through the article quickly and find the phrases from Exercise 2. Did you combine the words in the same way?**

4 **Now read to find the answers to these questions.**

1 What does a courier do?
2 What are the advantages of being a courier?
3 What are the disadvantages?

PSST – Do you fancy a fortnight in Rio for only £200?

It could be yours if you're prepared to fly around the world as a courier, explains **Simon Calder**.

THE BEST job I've ever had was working for Securicor. It was so good that *I* paid *them*. The job lasted just seven hours,
5- half of which was spent hanging around baggage check-ins. The rest of the time I was 11 miles high, travelling at twice the speed of sound and
10- enjoying an excellent meal en route to New York. I flew the Atlantic on Concorde for £150.

Express delivery companies use couriers like me to provide
15- a fast service at low cost. The best way to send urgent documents is as accompanied baggage, but then a fare-paying passenger has to travel with
20- them. The companies would prefer to use their own staff; they are familiar with customs procedures and are reliable, but they are also expensive, as
25- salaries have to be added to the cost of fares. So it's much cheaper for the companies to use people off the street on a casual basis.
30-   There are drawbacks to using a courier flight for your holiday trip. The range of destinations is restricted; the dates of both the outward and return flights are fixed. It can -35 also be anti-social; since only one person is needed on most days, a couple must split up and travel on successive days or buy a full-fare ticket for one of -40 them.

The day of the flight is not without its problems. You must check in at least two hours in advance, and look -45 reasonably smart – no jeans or training shoes. Steady nerves are necessary: you must not be too alarmed if the company's representatives -50 show up with only 30 minutes remaining. You may find yourself with loads of hand luggage, especially if television companies are keen -55 to get video tapes across the Atlantic quickly.

But Susan Griffiths, author of *Work Your Way Around the World*, says that becoming a -60 regular and reliable casual courier can be valuable. 'The company may start coming up with some real last-minute bargains – one reader told me -65 he had been offered a fortnight in Rio for £200!'

5 Look at these adjectives:

excellent   restricted   steady
fast   fixed   low   anti-social
reliable   smart   expensive

1   Which nouns do they refer to in the article?
2   In the context of the article, are they positive or negative qualities?

LISTENING

6 Before you listen, look at the advertisement below and answer the questions.

ICS

*delivers your parcels
to any place
at any time*

• DOOR TO DOOR • LOW PRICES
• COMPLETE SECURITY

Call free:
UK deliveries 0800 121212
International 0800 121213

---

1   What is the name of the company?
2   What does the company do?
3   What number do you phone if you are in London and you have a parcel for New York?
4   What exactly do you think the company will do after you phone them?

7 📼 Listen to a conversation between an employee of a delivery company and a client.

1   What is the woman planning to send?
2   Where is the parcel going to go to and from?
3   How long will it take?

8 📼 Listen again and note down:

1   the information that the company needs before the parcel is collected.
2   what the driver has to do when he collects the parcel.
3   what the sender has to write on the customs invoice.

DISCOVERING LANGUAGE

9 Look at these examples of reported speech from the conversation:

> A *The manager says that there are daily flights at midday. The manager says we can collect the parcel from you at 10.15 ...*
>
> B *The airlines said that we'd have to check all parcels; they told us we had to do it.*

1   Are there any differences between the manager's original words and the reported speech?
2   What differences are there between the airline representative's words and the reported speech?
3   Why do you think there are tense changes in B and not in A?
4   Use Sentence B above to complete parts of the chart below. It shows how verb forms change in some uses of reported speech. Then use Text C below to complete the rest of the chart.

direct speech	reported speech
present simple	*past simple*
present progressive	.....
past simple	*past simple/.....*
present perfect	.....
past perfect	*past perfect*
will, can, may, must/have to	....
would, could, should, might	*would, could, should, might*

> C *I said to the woman at ICS that I had already phoned her and we were now waiting for the driver so that we could leave the office. She said that before the driver had left, he had reported engine trouble, so he might be late.*

10 Using your notes from Exercises 7 and 8, tell your partner in your own words what the person at the delivery company said about procedures.

11 Tell your partner about something interesting that has happened to you recently. Then tell your partner's story to another student, using reported speech. Tell the last story you hear to the person who first told it. Is it still accurate?

Focus

TOPIC
- Emergency services

FUNCTIONS
- Telephoning

SKILLS
- Listening: an interview, phone calls, a conversation
- Speaking: a role play, a report of a conversation

Emergency!

GETTING STARTED

1 Look at the pictures.

1 What do you think the woman's job is?
2 What sort of people do you think she usually speaks to on the phone?
3 What is the number for the emergency services in your country?
4 Have you ever rung that number? What happened when your call was answered?
5 Who are the people in uniform in Picture B? Describe the differences between what they are wearing and uniforms in your country.

🎞 Documentary

LISTENING

2 📼 Listen to an interview with Michelle Redfern, the woman in Picture A.

Part 1
1 Where does Michelle work?
2 What number do you dial for the emergency services in Britain?
3 Who will answer this call first?
4 What will that person ask you?
5 What does Michelle need to know first?
6 What is the next thing she asks about?
7 What help can she give on the phone?

Part 2
8 What did a doctor's receptionist tell Michelle earlier in the day?
9 What does Michelle say is the main purpose of her job?

SPEAKING

3 📼 Someone is calling an ambulance. Look at the parts of a conversation below.

1 Decide which ones are spoken by the caller (C), the British Telecom operator (BT), the Ambulance Service operator (AS).
   a) Can you spell that, please?
   b) Yes, there's been an accident ... a boy has been hit by a car.
   c) Emergency Services. Fire, police or ambulance?
   d) OK, we'll have an ambulance there as soon as possible.
   e) Can you tell me exactly where you are?
   f) I'm putting you through.
   g) Is the boy conscious?
   h) Ambulance, please.
   i) In Fulham, outside number ... 44, Birchfield Avenue.
   j) Hello. London Ambulance. Can I help you?
   k) B-I-R-C-H-F-I-E-L-D. Birchfield.
   l) Yes, but he's losing a lot of blood.

2 Put the conversation in the correct order, and then listen and check.

4 Work in groups of three and role play the situations below. Change roles so that everyone plays each part.

Student A: You are the British Telecom operator. Ask Student C which service they want and put them through to Student B.

Student B: You are the operator for one of the emergency services. Ask Student C for the information you need to send help.

Student C: Phone the emergency services to deal with these situations:

a) a small child in the river
b) a robbery in a shop
c) a fire at your home

↻ COMPARING CULTURES

5 Think about conventions for answering the phone.

1 Look at this extract from the opening of a telephone conversation:

MARK: Five-six-four, two-one-oh. Hello?
CLARA: Is that Mark?
MARK: Yes.
CLARA: Oh. This is Clara, I'm a friend of Jean-Pierre ...

Do you group telephone numbers in the same way in your language? In what ways would this conversation be different in your language?

2 Read a second extract.

WOMAN: Hello, can I speak to Mr Naylor, please?
MAN: Speaking.

Who is the man in this conversation? What is the full form of the phrase *Speaking*? How would this conversation be different in your language?

FOCUS ON FUNCTIONS

6 📼 Listen to and read this telephone conversation. Match the functions below to parts of the conversation.

RECEPTIONIST: Good morning, Prescott Publishing.
NURSE: Hello, could you put me through to Ms Bayliss, please?
REC: Certainly. *Who's calling?* [1]
NURSE: It's Staff Nurse Evans here. I'm calling from the hospital.
REC: *Hold the line, please* [2], *I'll put you through ...* [3] *Sorry to keep you waiting.* [4] *I'm afraid her line's engaged at the moment.* [5] *Would you like to leave a message?* [6]
NURSE: No, I'm afraid I need to speak to her immediately. It's urgent.
REC: Right. *Just a moment* [7] – I'll let her know ...

a) asking someone to wait (2)
b) explaining why you can't connect the call
c) apologising for the delay
d) asking who the caller is
e) saying you are going to connect the call
f) making a suggestion

7 Think about the language of telephoning in Exercise 6.

1 Can you think of other ways of asking someone to wait?
   Hold on ...

2 What other reasons might there be for not connecting a call?
   I'm afraid she's in a meeting.

3 Why does the receptionist use *I'll* to say what he is going to do?

4 What other suggestions could the receptionist make?
   Shall I ask her to call you?

8 Work in pairs.

Student A: You need to speak to Mr Pearson urgently. Decide why and then ring him.

Student B: You are Mr Pearson's secretary. He does not want any calls, so make excuses for him but be very polite.

Then change roles. This time, Mr Pearson is out.

LISTENING

9 📼 Listen to the conversation between the nurse and Ms Bayliss.

1 Who is in hospital?
2 What happened to him?
3 What are his injuries?
4 Is he in danger?
5 How long will he be in hospital?
6 What is Ms Bayliss going to do now?

10 Work in pairs. It is the day after Helen Bayliss's son had an accident, and she is back at work.

Student A: You are Helen. Tell your colleague about the phone call from the hospital.

Student B: You are Helen's colleague. Ask questions.

HELEN: *I had a terrible shock. I got a phone call from the hospital.*
COLLEAGUE: *What about?*
HELEN: *My son. They told me he **had had** an accident.*
COLLEAGUE: ...

Short reports

Focus

↻ COMPARING CULTURES

1 What percentage of teenagers in your country do you think are able to use computers at home? What do they use them for? List all the possibilities.

READING

2 Before you read, look at the newspaper headline. What do you think the article tells us about computer use among teenage girls and boys?

3 Read the article and check your answer to Exercise 2. What reasons are given for the differences in computer use between the sexes? What are the possible effects of these differences?

Girls just wanna have fun with learning, but boys will be game boys

GIRLS need much more encouragement from their parents if they are not to be left behind by the Information Technology revolution, a report from the National Council for Educational Technology suggests. Girls are thirteen times less likely than boys to have access to a computer at home.

The research shows that children who use a computer at home become more confident and enthusiastic about IT at school, but that advantage is especially marked among girls. Using a computer at home has a positive effect on girls' attitudes to IT in all areas.

Parents need to be aware that girls react differently to the IT revolution. They are not attracted by many of the video games that obsess the boys and they particularly dislike the violence and sexual stereotyping of some of the games.

Girls are attracted by the most useful aspects of IT – by word processors and databases. Given the right software at home, they can increase their capability and enthusiasm and may be able to redress some of the imbalance between the sexes on higher-level computing courses at schools and colleges.

DEVELOPING VOCABULARY

4 Look at the use of these verbs from the article:

suggests (para. 1)   *shows* (para. 2)

1 Which verb refers to a more definite conclusion?

2 Which of these verbs and verb phrases have a similar meaning to *suggest*? Which are more like *show*?
prove   indicate   imply   demonstrate
confirm   provide some evidence
provide conclusive evidence

READING

5 Read this report on a survey of computer use in a group of young people.

1 Match these titles to the paragraphs:
RESULTS 1   INTRODUCTION   CONCLUSION
CARRYING OUT THE SURVEY   RESULTS 2

2 What questions were people asked? Draw up a questionnaire.

3 What do the different bars in the chart show? There is one mistake in the chart. What is it?

■ At home with computers

This report presents details of home computer use by a sample group of young people. It is a common belief that teenagers today know about computers and are familiar with using them in all aspects of their lives. We decided to try to find out if this was true.

We questioned thirty young people between 14 and 18. All the teenagers we chose said they had computers at home. We asked them how much time they spent on their computer in an average week, but we were most interested in what they used their computers for.

The average time spent on a computer in a week was about 12 hours, with the highest user averaging 32 hours and the lowest user only 5 hours. There was no significant difference between boys and girls.

All of the people questioned said they regularly used the computer to play games. Fourteen told us they did some

FOCUS ON FUNCTIONS

6 Look back at the report. Which tense of the verb is used:

a) when the subject is *the report, the results* or *the chart*?

b) to describe how the survey was carried out?

c) to report results?

d) to present conclusions?

Which other structure is common in the reporting of results?

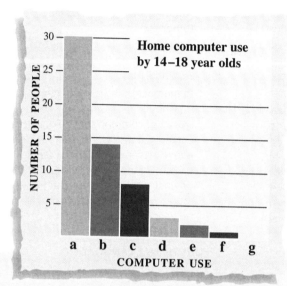

Home computer use by 14–18 year olds

NUMBER OF PEOPLE

30 — 25 — 20 — 15 — 10 — 5 —

a b c d e f g

COMPUTER USE

word-processing at home, but not very much. Only 2 of the respondents said that computers helped them with their studies, while 8 people told us they kept addresses and telephone numbers on their computers or used them as diaries. Only 3 people said they were learning to program computers, and nobody consulted databases (other than their address lists). None of the people used their computer for any other purpose. The chart gives the overall results in detail.

The results indicate that average computer use is quite high amongst 14-18 year olds. They also show quite clearly that computers are seen by most young people as little more than games machines. The only other significant uses are for word-processing and organising address lists. It seems to us that, although computers are common in the homes of British adolescents, they have not yet become useful tools in the routine of everyday life.

7 How many different words and phrases does the writer use to refer to the people who were questioned during the survey? Why do you think the writer uses different expressions in the report?

SPEAKING

8 Work in small groups. Look at your questionnaires from Exercise 5.

1 You are going to carry out a survey of home computer use by people in your class. Are there any questions you would like to change or add? Do you, for example, need to ask about work rather than studies?

2 Use copies of your questionnaire to interview your classmates. Then return to your group and assemble your results.

WRITING

9 Write a report presenting your findings. Use the same structure as the report in Exercise 5.

10 After writing your first draft:

1 check that the structure of the report matches the one in Exercise 5.

2 try to improve the vocabulary you have used. If you can, avoid repeating the same words and phrases.

3 check the grammar of your sentences, particularly where you have used reported speech.

Language reference

GRAMMAR

Reported speech

We use reported speech to refer to a statement or question that we or another person made earlier.
EXAMPLE: *He said he was going to London.*

1 Reporting verbs

- The most common reporting verbs are:
  say (that) + reported statement   EXAMPLE: *I **said (that)** I'd be there.*
  tell someone (that) + reported statement
  EXAMPLE: *I **told her (that)** I'd be there.*
  ask someone if/when/where, etc. + reported question
  EXAMPLE: *I **asked her if** she'd be there.*

- There are many other reporting verbs, e.g. *inform, report, enquire.* You need to check the structure that follows each one in your dictionary.

2 Present tense reporting verbs

- When the reporting verb is in a present tense (e.g. present simple, present perfect), the tense of the verb in the reported speech stays the same as in the original statement.

- Pronouns change if necessary to keep the same sense, and the verb always agrees with the new subject pronoun.
  Direct speech   'I'm going to India.'
  Reported speech   *She says/has said that she is going to India.*

3 Past tense reporting verbs

- When the reporting verb is in a past tense (e.g. past simple, past perfect), the tense of the verb in the reported speech usually changes. Changes reflect a change in perspective, and they make the original speech distant from the present.
  Direct speech   'I **love** spaghetti.'
  Reported speech   *He said he **loved** spaghetti.*

- Where appropriate, verb forms change as follows:

DIRECT SPEECH	REPORTED SPEECH
present simple	→ past simple
present progressive	→ past progressive
past simple	→ past simple/past perfect
past progressive	→ past/past perfect progressive
present perfect	→ past perfect
present perfect progressive	→ past perfect progressive
past perfect	→ past perfect (no change)
can, will, may, must/have to	→ could, would, might, had to
could, would, might, should	→ could, would, might, should (no change)

- Other changes that are often necessary after a past tense reporting verb are changes to:
  pronouns
  Direct speech   'Have **you** seen John?'
  Reported speech   *We asked if **he/she/Tim/Sara** had seen John.*

possessives
Direct speech   'Is the case **yours**?'
Reported speech   *He asked if the case was **his/hers/Tim's/Sara's**.*

adverbials of place and time
now → *then*
today → *that day*
yesterday → *the day before*
here → *there*
Direct speech   'We'll be **here tomorrow**.'
Reported speech   *They said they'd be **there the next/following day**.*

Remember that these changes may not be necessary; they are a matter of common sense. For example, if the last reporter above was speaking on the same day and in the same place as the original speaker, the correct report would be *They said they'd be **here tomorrow**.*

FUNCTIONAL LANGUAGE

1 Reporting speech

I asked them when they would be free.

2 Using the telephone

ANSWERING THE PHONE
231 8842./Good morning. Prescott Publishing.

INTRODUCING YOURSELF
This is Clara.

ASKING WHO THE CALLER IS
Is that Mark?

SAYING WHO YOU WANT TO TALK TO
Hello. Can I speak to Mr Green, please?/Hello. Could you put me through to Mr Green, please?

SAYING YOU ARE CONNECTING THE
CALL *I'll put you through.*

ASKING SOMEONE TO WAIT
Hold the line, please./Hold on, please./Just a moment.

EXPLAINING THE DELAY
I'm afraid the line's engaged.

MAKING A SUGGESTION *Would you like to leave a message?*

Talkback

The truth game

Prepare to play the truth game!

1 Read the story below. What questions could you ask the man to find out if he is lying or telling the truth? Work with a partner and make a list of questions that you would like to ask.

When I was eleven, I was in a Hollywood film. An American film company was making a film in my town and they needed a young boy to play a small part – and I got it!

2 Work in groups of three, and choose one of these topics:
- an embarrassing experience
- a frightening event
- a lucky experience
- my greatest achievement
- a famous person that I have met
- an exciting journey
- something important that I have lost
- the strangest place that I have ever been to

Together, prepare three stories. One of you is going to tell a true story about a real experience that happened to you. Two of you are going to tell stories that are not true. Other students will question you about your stories, so make sure you have thought about the details.

3 Join with another group of three students. Listen to their stories and ask them questions. Think about which person is telling the truth and which people are lying. Then tell your stories and answer questions about them.

4 In your original group of three, discuss the stories that you heard. What did each person say? How convincing were they? What reasons can you give to support your view? Decide who was telling the truth and ask the other group if you are correct. Your group scores a point if you were right.

5 Choose another topic and play the game again. The group with the most points at the end wins the game.

15 *A change of scene*

Preparing to leave

Focus

TOPICS
- Preparations for travel
- Working holidays

GRAMMAR
- First conditional
- Conjunctions: *if, unless, when, as soon as*

SKILLS
- Speaking: discussion
- Reading: an article

GETTING STARTED

1 Imagine that you have been employed to lead a group of teenagers on a coach trip to a number of different countries. You will stay in cheap hotels and do a lot of walking in towns and countryside.

1 Work with a partner and write a packing list. Use these headings to help you:
DOCUMENTS: *insurance certificate, . . .*
CLOTHES: *walking boots, . . .*
TOILETRIES & MEDICINES: *toothbrush, . . .*
EQUIPMENT: *compass, . . .*
BOOKS: *guidebooks, . . .*
OTHER THINGS: *towel, . . .*

2 Your bag is too heavy to carry. Agree with your partner which items you can leave out from each of your bags. Explain to another pair of students why the things in your bag now are essential. Do they agree?

READING

2 Discuss these questions in groups.

1 Have you or has anyone you know ever been on a working holiday? What kind of job was it? Where was it? Did you/your friend enjoy it?

2 What sort of jobs do you think students can find if they want to work abroad during the summer holidays? Make a list: *tour guide, waiter, . . .*

3 Read the article and compare the information with your answers to Exercise 2 above.

WORKING HOLIDAYS

■ Every summer, hundreds of thousands of students travel to other countries looking for work and adventure. Most of the opportunities are in seasonal work, mainly
5- connected with tourism and agriculture. The pay is usually poor, but most people work abroad for the thrill of travel. You can pick grapes in France, work on a family campsite, entertain kids on American
10- summer camps, and, of course, there are always jobs in hotels and restaurants.

■ But it is not as easy as it used to be to find work. 'Unless you speak the language of the country well, there will be very few
15- openings,' says Anthea Ellis, an adviser on vacation work for students. 'If you work as a nanny with a family in Italy, then of course you'll have to speak Italian. When you arrive to wash dishes in a restaurant in Paris, the
20- owner will expect you to speak French.

SPEAKING

4 Look back at the article and discuss these questions.

1 What are the advantages and disadvantages of this kind of work?
2 What kind of person do you think you need to be to do Sarah James' job?
3 List the kinds of work mentioned in the article. Which would you most/least like to do? What exactly do you think your responsibilities would be?

5 Explain the meaning of these phrases from the article:

1 *seasonal work*	What seasonal work is available in your area?
2 *the thrill of travel*	Do you experience this feeling? Explain why (not).
3 *casual work*	Is this available to people locally? What can they do?
4 *employment rights*	Can you give examples from your own country?
5 *to get the sack*	What can lead to this in your/a friend's job?

British students only have a language advantage for jobs in the USA and Australia.'

■ Not everyone enjoys the experience. Sarah James was a courier responsible for forty American children in Europe. The two -25 teachers who accompanied the children had never been abroad. One child lost his passport; another became seriously ill and was flown home; four children were lost in Madrid for a whole day; the whole group was thrown out of -30 one hotel because of the noise they made, and Sarah herself was mugged on her only free evening of the entire trip. 'I did visit a lot of new places,' she says, 'but it wasn't worth it. The pay was awful and it really was a 24-hour- -35 a-day job. The kids never slept!'

■ 'The trouble is, students expect to have an easy time of it,' Anthea Ellis points out. 'After all, they see it as a holiday. In practice, though, you have to work hard. At the same time, all -40 vacation work is *casual* work. You'll have a job when the hotel, the restaurant, or the campsite is busy. In other words, you'll work if it's convenient for the company that employs you. But you have few employment rights. -45 As soon as the holiday season finishes, they'll get rid of you. If you don't work hard, or if your employer doesn't like you, you'll get the sack.'

DISCOVERING LANGUAGE

6 Look back at the article.

1 Find first conditional sentences. Remind yourself of the structure and the use of the first conditional: *If . . .*
2 Find sentences with a similar structure that begin with these words:
   a) *unless*   b) *when*   c) *as soon as*
3 What are the differences in meaning between:
   a) *if* and *unless*?   b) *when* and *as soon as*?
4 Each sentence containing these conjunctions has two clauses. If you change the order of the clauses, is there any difference in meaning?

7 ▭ A woman is reading some advice for students from an organisation that arranges worldwide employment. Her teenage son is responding. Listen to the example, and then give appropriate responses to the other pieces of advice. Compare your answers with the conversation on the cassette.

MOTHER: You'll contact your employers immediately, won't you?
SON: *Don't worry! I'll contact them as soon as I arrive.*

ADVICE FOR STUDENTS

- Contact your employer on arrival. — (as soon as)
- Look after your bags in public places. — (if)
- Do not eat unwashed fruit. — (unless)
- Boil all water outside the cities. — (if)
- Take your malaria tablets every morning. — (when)
- Let your family know your new address. — (when)
- Start learning the local language immediately. — (as soon as)
- Do not accept invitations from complete strangers. — (unless)

8 Work in groups and discuss advice that you would give a foreign student who wants to work in your area. Give reasons for your advice.

A: *It's important to dress properly here.*
B: *Yes, if your clothes are too informal, your colleagues won't respect you.*

Getting away

↻ COMPARING CULTURES

1 The most popular holiday destinations for British tourists are:

Spain   Greece   the United States
Portugal   France

1 What are the most popular foreign holiday destinations for people from your country? Why do you think these places are so popular?

2 Work in groups of four. Agree on your top five holiday destinations and explain your choice to the class.

2 Where do visitors to your own country come from? Which are the most popular destinations for foreign tourists?

🖼 Documentary

LISTENING

3 Before you listen, look at photographs from a holiday brochure. What kind of holidays do you think the company specialises in?

4 📼 Listen to Maria Paul, a travel agent, talking about her work. Check your answers to Exercise 3 and answer these questions.

1 What kind of accommodation does the island of Kurumba offer?
   a) cheap   b) expensive
   c) very expensive

2 Is Kurumba in:
   a) the Caribbean?
   b) the Maldive Islands?
   c) Thailand?

3 How can clients travel around the Caribbean?
   a) on a ship   b) by plane   c) by coach

4 Which four destinations does Maria mention as the most popular with her clients?

Focus

TOPIC
• Holidays

GRAMMAR
• Indirect questions
• Embedded questions

FUNCTIONS
• Asking politely

SKILLS
• Speaking: discussion, role play
• Listening: a monologue, a conversation at a travel agent's
• Writing: form completion

5 📼 **Listen to the first part of a conversation in a travel agency. A couple are booking a holiday.**

1 Where are they going?
2 How long are they going for?
3 How will they travel?
4 How many cities will they visit?
5 What time of day will they leave Britain?
6 Which of these are included in the price of the holiday?
  a) hotels   c) transport from the airport to the
  b) meals   hotel
             d) travel insurance

WRITING

6 📼 **Complete as much of the booking form as you can. Then listen to the whole conversation and fill in the other details.**

BOOKING FORM

Names of travellers

Surname	Initials	Mr/Ms
....	....	....
....	....	....

Telephone
Home: ....   Office: ....

Travel details

Outward   Date ....   Time ....
           From ....   To ....
           Airline ....

Return   Date ....   Time ....
           From ....   To ....
           Airline ....

Accommodation

Hotel name ...... *Pullman Maadi Towers.*
           Number of nights ....

Boat name ....
           Number of nights ....

Deposit   ...... people at £100 each = £ ....
Insurance ...... people at ..... each = £ ....

FOCUS ON FUNCTIONS

7 Look at these lines from the conversation:

A *Do you know what the flight times are?*
B *Can you tell me if you need travel insurance?*
C *I can't remember what you include in the price.*
D *I wonder if I could take some details now.*
E *I don't know when you want to pay the balance of the holiday price.*

1 Why do we use indirect questions like A and B?
2 Make A and B more direct. What changes are necessary?
3 Are C–E statements or questions:
  a) grammatically?   b) functionally?
4 Change C–E into direct questions. What changes are necessary?

8 Use the prompts to make the questions below more polite in different ways.

When does the plane leave?
Do you know when the plane leaves?
I don't know when the plane leaves.

1 How much does this cost?
  Could you ...   I wonder ...
2 Which airport do you want to leave from?
  Can you ...   I don't know ...
3 Do you want a luxury hotel?
  Can you ...   I can't remember ...
4 Would you like to hire a car?
  Do you know ...   I don't know ...
5 When will you be able to pay the balance?
  Do you know ...   I wonder ...

SPEAKING

9 Work in pairs.

Student A: You have booked a holiday to Thailand and you have come into the travel agency to collect your tickets. You have lost the information that you were given about the holiday. Ask the travel agent, as politely as possible, for the information below.

A: (which airport/leave?)
  Can you tell me which airport I leave from?
  I can't remember which airport I leave from.

1 time/outward flight?
2 how much/baggage allowance?
3 when/arrive/Bangkok?
4 name/hotel?
5 how many days/holiday?
6 already/book/car?
7 all meals/hotel?
8 need/visa?

Student B: You work at the travel agency. Turn to page 128 and give the information that your partner asks for.

Persuasion

Focus

TOPICS
- Persuasion
- Travel brochures

SKILLS
- Reading: persuasive and neutral texts
- Writing: a persuasive description

VOCABULARY DEVELOPMENT
- Adjectives: degrees of intensity

READING

1 Look at extracts A–C.

1 Where are they from?
2 Who are they written for?
3 What is the writer's purpose in each case?

A

AS WE RACE FOR THE FUTURE WE HAVEN'T FORGOTTEN THE PAST.

Garuda Indonesia
THE AIRLINE OF INDONESIA

B

Colourful photographs and evocative prose are combined with the kind of insider's information, local trivia, do-it-yourself walks and excursions and detailed practical information that make travelling a delight.
Both independent travellers and package tourists will find

C

and I do hope you'll join me here for your holiday. I know the flights are expensive, but the cost of living is low here and you'd be able to stay with me while you're in Surabaya. I can't tell you how exciting it is to travel around the islands, visiting

2 What information would you expect to find in an extract from a travel brochure? List qualities of a place that are attractive to you.

natural beauty, …

3 Read Extract D below.

1 Who would normally read this? Why?
2 How many of the qualities on your list from Exercise 2 are mentioned here? Are there any that are not on your list?

D Bali is blessed with radiant sunshine, a fresh verdant landscape, beautiful sunsets and dazzling white beaches. Visitors from all over the world come to immerse themselves in the delights of the stunning mountain scenery and the clear blue lake and sea waters. In the vibrant coastal resorts are high-quality modern hotels and an exciting nightlife to take you through till dawn, but behind the bright lights you will find a traditional way of life that has thrived for centuries. The spectacular temples, the colourful ritual dances, the shadow puppet plays, the vast range of handicrafts all show the strength and vitality of the local culture. The friendly and gentle Balinese will welcome you to share their island – and you will want to return again and again to this unique paradise on earth.

4 Work with a partner.

1 Put these topics in the order in which they occur in the text.
   a) local culture   c) people
   b) nature/climate   d) modern facilities
2 Make a list of all the words and phrases in the extract that relate to each of the topics.

5 Use a dictionary to help you with the activities below.

1 Extract D is full of language that expresses the writer's opinion. What do these adjectives mean? Can you think of more neutral alternatives?
   a) radiant *bright*
   b) verdant   e) vibrant
   c) dazzling   f) spectacular
   d) stunning   g) vast

2 Replace these verb phrases from the text with more neutral phrases.
   a) is blessed
   b) immerse themselves in
   c) has thrived
   d) to share

3 Think of more neutral alternatives for these nouns and noun phrases.
   a) landscape   b) delights
   c) paradise on earth

4 The writer also gives an impression of spirituality. Find four words or phrases in the text that help to give this impression.

5 Read the extract again and rewrite each sentence so that all the writer's opinions are removed. Leave only the bare facts. Rephrase the sentences in any way you like.
   Bali is sunny and green with lots of beaches.

DEVELOPING VOCABULARY

6 Look at the common adjectives below.

1 How many alternatives can you think of for each one?
   a) good *wonderful, excellent…*
   b) bad   f) small
   c) hot   g) attractive
   d) cold   h) ugly
   e) big

2 Now put the alternatives for each adjective in order of intensity.
   good: *not bad – nice – great – excellent/ fantastic/wonderful*

WRITING

7 Work in pairs. Look at the text below, which does not contain any persuasive language. Make it more persuasive by following the guidelines. The first sentence of the text has been used as an example.

1 Add adjectives.

  wonderful, golden
Rio de Janeiro has 56 miles of ⎰ beaches and has high

temperatures for most of the year.

2 Improve nouns and other adjectives.

Rio de Janeiro has 56 miles of wonderful, golden beaches
  glorious sunshine
and has ~~high temperatures~~ for most of the year.

3 Add words, phrases and clauses. Improve verbs.

The beautiful city of , the cultural capital of Brazil,
  ⎰Rio de Janeiro⎰ has 56 miles of wonderful, golden beaches
  enjoys
and ~~has~~ glorious sunshine for most of the year.

Rio de Janeiro

Rio de Janeiro has 56 miles of beaches and has high temperatures for most of the year. People come to Rio to sail and swim in the sea, and to walk in the hills and mountains that overlook the city. It is known for its shopping, its international restaurants and its nightlife. Carnival time is in February but you can visit the local 'samba' schools at any time of the year. Tourists are welcome in Brazil, where the people are friendly.

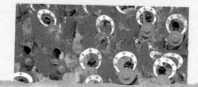

8 Write persuasively about a place in your country – perhaps the place where you live – so that any reader will *certainly want to* visit the place.

Language reference

GRAMMAR

1 Indirect questions

USE

- Indirect questions are usually used to be more formal or polite. Compare these questions:

  Direct question   *What's the time, please?*
  Indirect question   *Can you tell me what the time is, please?*

FORMS

- Introductory phrases for indirect questions include *Can you tell me ...?* and *Do you know ...?* The word order that follows these phrases is the same as for a statement.

  COMPARE: *Where **is the bank**?* (verb – subject)
  *Can you tell me where **the bank is**?*
  (subject – verb)

- To make a *wh* question more polite, use an introductory phrase + *wh* word + subject + verb.
  EXAMPLE: ***Can you tell me where** the bank is?*

- To make other questions more polite, use an introductory phrase + *if* + subject + verb.
  EXAMPLE: ***Do you know if** the bank is open?*

2 Embedded questions

USES

- Embedded questions can be simple statements of fact.
  EXAMPLE: *She can't remember how she got home.*

- They can also have the same function as indirect questions.
  EXAMPLE: *I don't know which terminal my flight leaves from.* (= Can you tell me ... ?)

FORMS

- Embedded questions have a similar structure to indirect questions, i.e. the word order after the introductory phrase is like a statement. Introductory phrases include verbs like *remember, know* and *wonder*.
  EXAMPLE: *I **wonder** who Pete's new girlfriend is.*

3 *Unless*

- Like *if*, *unless* is often used in first conditional structures. It has a similar meaning to *if ... not*.
  EXAMPLE: *We won't go **unless** you come too.* (= We won't go **if** you **don't** come too, *or* We'll **only** go **if** you come too.)

- However, *unless* is not identical to *if ... not*. *Unless* is used to introduce the *only* condition for a possible future event or state. It emphasises the meaning *except if ...*.
  EXAMPLE: ***Unless** we meet tomorrow, I'll see you on Thursday.* (= I'll *only* see you on Thursday if there is no meeting tomorrow.)
  To express other meanings, we use *if ... not*.

4 *When* and *as soon as*

- These are both time conjunctions. *As soon as* has the more precise meaning of *immediately/at the moment when*.

- These conjunctions are used to introduce time clauses in sentences which have the same structure as the conditional sentences in 3 above.
  EXAMPLES: *I'll ring you **when** I get home. **As soon as** I get home, I'll ring you.*

- *When* and *as soon as* refer to a future event in sentences like this, but they are followed by a present simple verb. *Will* marks the future in the main clause.

FUNCTIONAL LANGUAGE

Asking polite questions
Can you tell me where Terminal 1 is?
I wonder if you can help me.

Progress check Units 14–15

GRAMMAR AND FUNCTIONS

1 Complete the paragraph below. Fill each gap with the correct form of the verb in brackets or one of these words:

if   unless   when   as soon as

'¹..... you ²..... (arrive), someone will be at the airport to meet you. ³..... she ⁴..... (not be) in the Arrivals Hall, she'll be at the information desk. She ⁵..... (show) you the taxi rank ⁶..... you prefer to catch a bus into town. ⁷..... you ⁸..... (take) a taxi, the fare will be on the meter. The taxi driver will probably speak English ⁹..... you ¹⁰..... (want) to practise your French. ¹¹..... you arrive at the hotel, the reception staff ¹²..... (need) to see your booking form. You'll want to change money ¹³..... you ¹⁴..... (can). There are facilities in all the big hotels but ¹⁵..... you can wait, you ¹⁶..... (get) a better exchange rate from a bank.'

2 Read this telephone conversation. A woman is phoning the hotel reception desk from her room. Make the words in *italics* more polite.

RECEPTIONIST: *Yes?*

CLIENT: Good afternoon. *I want to speak to the manager.*

RECEPTIONIST: *He's not here.*

CLIENT: *Where is he?*

RECEPTIONIST: I'm sorry, I don't know.

CLIENT: *Connect me with his secretary, then.*

RECEPTIONIST: *What's your name?*

CLIENT: My name's Langley. Clare Langley.

RECEPTIONIST: OK. *Wait.*

3 Combine each pair of sentences into one, using embedded questions.

1 Does it rain in Morocco in January? I don't know. *I don't know ...*
2 Do you need a visa? I can't remember.
3 Which is the best hotel in Casablanca? I wonder.
4 Where can you ski? I'll find out.
5 Which currency do they use? I know.

4 Read the direct speech and then correct the reported speech so that it is accurate.

1 'It rains in coastal areas. It doesn't rain much in Marrakesh.'
   She said it was raining in coastal areas, but that it wasn't raining much in Marrakesh.
2 'I've asked the embassy about visas.'
   She said that I had asked the embassy about visas.
3 'Can you check the hotels in your guidebook tomorrow?'
   Last week she asked me if I can check the hotels in her guidebook tomorrow.
4 'We're planning to go into the Atlas Mountains.'
   She told me that they have planned to go into the Atlas Mountains.
5 'I'll ask about money. We probably can't buy Moroccan dirhams here.'
   Before they left, she said that she will ask about money. She said that they probably can't buy Moroccan dirhams there.

VOCABULARY

5 Complete the questions with a suitable adjective.

How *hot* was it? It was boiling!

1 How ..... was the desert? It was vast!
2 How ..... were the mountains? They were spectacular!
3 How ..... was the sun? It was dazzling!
4 How ..... was the food? It was wonderful!
5 How ..... was the sea? It was freezing!
6 How ..... was your sunburn? It was awful.

Exercises for Student B

Unit 3: Coming and going, Exercise 12

You are passing through Customs. Your partner has found these parcels. Look at the contents, then use your imagination to answer your partner's questions.

Unit 7: An unusual break, Exercise 8

Answer your partner's questions. Then look at the words below and ask questions to help your partner guess them.

B: *What do you call a person who works with wood?*
A: *A person who works with wood is called a carpenter.*

carpenter   driving licence   bicycle   shelf
journalist   typewriter

Unit 10: Stages, Exercise 6

You work in a theatre box office. Look at the details of performances below. Give your customer the information he/she wants and sell him/her some tickets.

New Theatre, Shaftesbury Avenue			
Day	Programme	Time	Availability
Mon	LOVE BOAT	8.00 p.m.	all prices
Tues	LOVE BOAT	8.00 p.m.	all prices
Wed	MACBETH	2.30 p.m.	stalls/upper circle
		8.00 p.m.	sold out
Thurs	MACBETH	8.00 p.m.	all except front stalls
Fri	MACBETH	8.00 p.m.	back stalls
Sat	MACBETH	2.30 p.m.	all prices
		8.00 p.m.	sold out
Sun	CLOSED		

Prices: front stalls and circle £15   back stalls £12
upper circle £10

10% discount for students and pensioners, and for afternoon performances

Unit 13: Learning experiences, Exercise 11

You work at the museum. Look at the museum plan and give your partner directions. Use the expressions below to help you. Then change roles and turn back to page 107.

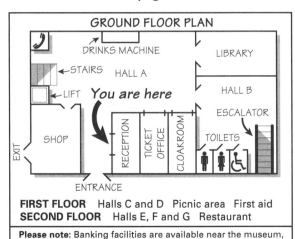

FIRST FLOOR   Halls C and D   Picnic area   First aid
SECOND FLOOR   Halls E, F and G   Restaurant

Please note: Banking facilities are available near the museum, opposite the main entrance.

Useful expressions

It's
They're
| upstairs.
| downstairs.
| on the (second) floor.
| near the entrance.

Go up the escalator to ...
Take the lift to the ... floor.
You can use the stairs.

Unit 15: Getting away, Exercise 9

You work in a travel agency. Look at the details below and give your partner the information he/she needs. Start like this:

Good morning/afternoon. Can I help you?

TRAVEL DETAILS			
Outward			
Date: 16/3	Depart: 16.45	Airport: Heathrow	
Airline: Thai	Arrive: 05.50	Airport: Bangkok	
Return			
Date: 26/3	Depart: 08.30	Airport: Bangkok	
Airline: Thai	Arrive: 15.15	Airport: Heathrow	
ACCOMMODATION			
Hotel name:	Caledonian (Bed and breakfast only)		
Number of nights:	10		
Car hire:	No		
Visa requirement:	Yes		
Baggage allowance:	20kg		